A READING GUIDE TO THE BOOK OF MORMON

DAVID H. MULHOLLAND

Deseret Book Company
Salt Lake City, Utah

To David, John, Brian, Sarah, Roger, and Matthew

My thanks to—
My wife, Lois, and our children for allowing me the time necessary to write
and for their helpful suggestions.
Allen J. and Elaine Fletcher for their thoughtful review and helpful suggestions.

© 1989 David H. Mulholland
All rights reserved.
Printed in the United States of America

No part of this book may be reproduced in any form
or by any means without permission in writing from the publisher,
Deseret Book Company, P.O. Box 30178, Salt Lake City, Utah 84130.

This work is not an official publication of
The Church of Jesus Christ of Latter-day Saints.
The views expressed herein are the responsibility of the author
and do not necessarily represent the position of the Church or of Deseret Book Company.

Deseret Book is a registered trademark of Deseret Book Company.

ISBN 0-87579-183-2

3   5   7   9   10   8   6   4   2

Contents

Preface

This guide will help you to better understand and apply in your own life the teachings of the Book of Mormon prophets. Our modern prophet, President Ezra Taft Benson, in his first general conference address as President of The Church of Jesus Christ of Latter-day Saints, spoke strongly of the need for members of the Church to study the Book of Mormon every day and of the rewards we would receive for doing so. He quoted Elder Marion G. Romney as follows:

"And so, I counsel you, my beloved brothers and sisters and friends everywhere, to make reading in the Book of Mormon a few minutes each day a lifelong practice. . . .

"I feel certain that if, in our homes, parents will read from the Book of Mormon prayerfully and regularly, both by themselves and with their children, the spirit of that great book will come to permeate our homes and all who dwell therein. The spirit of reverence will increase; mutual respect and consideration for each other will grow. The spirit of contention will depart. Parents will counsel their children in greater love and wisdom. Children will be more responsive and submissive to that counsel. Righteousness will increase. Faith, hope, and charity—the pure love of Christ—will abound in our homes and lives, bringing in their wake peace, joy, and happiness." (Conference Report, Apr. 1960, pp. 112–13, as cited in *Ensign*, May 1986, p. 6.)

Even more recently President Benson reemphasized the urgency of our need to study the Book of Mormon every day and then to share it with our neighbors:

"We need to read daily from the pages of the book that will get a man 'nearer to God by abiding by its precepts, than by any other book.' (*History of the Church*, 4:461.) . . .

"I challenge all of us to prayerfully consider steps that we can personally take to bring this new witness for Christ more fully into our own lives and into a world that so desperately needs it." (*Ensign,* Nov. 1988, pp. 4–6.)

The Nephite prophets saw our day and directed their message to us. (See Mormon 8:35.) These prophets included in their record gospel principles that are important for us to know and apply in our lives.

As you study this sacred record, remember the words of Nephi:

"I did liken all scriptures unto us, that it might be for our profit and learning." (1 Nephi 19:23.)

To fully understand the message of the Book of Mormon, you should also follow the counsel of Moroni:

"And when ye shall receive these things, I would exhort you that ye would ask God, the Eternal Father, in the name of Christ, if these things are not true; and if ye shall ask with a sincere heart, with real intent, having faith in Christ, he will manifest the truth of it unto you, by the power of the Holy Ghost.

"And by the power of the Holy Ghost ye may know the truth of all things." (Moroni 10:4–5.)

How to Use This Reading Guide

When you begin your study of the Book of Mormon, first read the chapter in the scriptures before you answer the questions in the guide.

Next, go back through the chapter you have just read, and write in the guide the answer and number of the verse or verses where the answer is found. (You will find most of the answers in the chapter you are reading in the Book of Mormon, but you will need to look for a few answers in other places in the scriptures.)

Then compare the verse or verses you wrote down with the verses listed in the Answers section at the back of this guide. The Answers section should be used as a guide; you may find some answers in other verses not listed there.

Reviewing the answers from your last study session before you continue and discussing with others what you have studied will also help you remember what you have learned.

The designation "See" after a question refers you to the passage where you will find the answer. This designation is used only when the answer is not in the chapter you are currently reading. For example, "See 2 Nephi 2:16*b*" after a question means that you will find all or part of the answer in footnote *b* to verse 16 of 2 Nephi 2.

The designation "See also" refers you to related information that is not necessarily part of the answer. For example, you may be referred to the Bible Dictionary, which is in the appendix to the Latter-day Saint edition of the King James Version of the Bible.

In addition to the scriptures and this guide, the *Book of Mormon Student Manual,* prepared by the Church Educational System and published by the Church of Jesus Christ of Latter-day Saints, will help you better understand the history and doctrine you are reading.

Book of Mormon Chronology

600 B.C.	Lehi leaves Jerusalem (1 Nephi 2)
About 589 B.C.	Lehi and his group arrive in the promised land (1 Nephi 18)
399 B.C.	The Nephites are righteous (Jarom)
About 200 B.C.	Zeniff returns to land of Lehi-Nephi (Mosiah 9)
About 148 B.C.	Abinadi is killed by King Noah (Mosiah 12)
About 124 B.C.	Mosiah becomes king (Mosiah 6)
About 120 B.C.	Alma arrives in the land of Zarahemla (Mosiah 24)
About 94 B.C.	An angel appears to Alma the Younger (Mosiah 27)
About 92 B.C.	The sons of Mosiah preach to the Lamanites (Mosiah 28)
91 B.C.	Alma and King Mosiah die (Mosiah 29)
About 82 B.C.	Alma the Younger and Amulek preach in the city of Ammonihah (Alma 9)
77 B.C.	Alma the Younger meets the sons of Mosiah (Alma 17)
73 B.C.	Moroni raises the title of liberty (Alma 46)
67 B.C.	The kingmen seek to control the government (Alma 51)

52 B.C.	A secret combination kills the chief judge (Helaman 1)
6 B.C.	Samuel the Lamanite prophesies (Helaman 13)
2 B.C.	Signs and wonders are given (Helaman 16)
A.D. 1	Christ is born (3 Nephi 1)
A.D. 17	The people gather for protection (3 Nephi 3)
A.D. 29–30	People divide into tribes (3 Nephi 7)
A.D. 34	Christ visits the people (3 Nephi 11)
A.D. 201	Pride develops (4 Nephi 1)
About A.D. 244	The wicked outnumber the righteous (4 Nephi 1)
A.D. 321	Mormon is told of the sacred records (Mormon 1)
A.D. 385	The Nephites are destroyed (Mormon 6)
About A.D. 421	Moroni completes his record (Moroni 10)

Questions about the Book of Mormon

Title Page

PARAGRAPH

_____ a. Who wrote the title page of the Book of Mormon?

_____ b. List three reasons why the Book of Mormon was written.

_____ c. Who are the Gentiles? (See Bible Dictionary, p. 679, s.v. "Gentiles.")

_____ d. Who are the Jews? (See Bible Dictionary, p. 713, s.v. "Jews.")

Introduction

PARAGRAPH

_____ a. What is the "crowning event recorded in the Book of Mormon"?

_____ b. What did Joseph Smith tell the brethren concerning this record?

_____ c. To whom will the Holy Ghost witness the truth of this record?

The Testimony of Three Witnesses and the Testimony of Eight Witnesses

PARAGRAPH

_____ a. What are two important differences between the Testimony of Three Witnesses and the Testimony of Eight Witnesses?

Testimony of the Prophet Joseph Smith

PARAGRAPH

_____ a. What was Joseph Smith doing at the time of Moroni's first visit? (See also Joseph Smith–History 1:29.)

_____ b. List ten things that Moroni told Joseph Smith during his visits.

PARAGRAPH

A Brief Explanation about the Book of Mormon

_____ a. What are the four kinds of metal plates spoken of in the Book of Mormon?

_____ b. In what year, approximately, did Moroni hide up the plates "unto the Lord"?

1 NEPHI

VERSE NUMBER

1 Nephi 1

_____ a. List six things we learn about Nephi in verse 1.

_____ b. How did Nephi know his record to be true?

_____ c. How old was Zedekiah when he began to reign? (See 2 Chronicles 36:10–20.)

_____ d. What happened as Lehi "prayed unto the Lord, yea, even with all his heart, in behalf of his people"? (1 Nephi 1:5.)

_____ e. Why did the Jews mock Lehi when he declared the things he had seen and heard?

_____ f. What will Nephi show you as you read his record?

---

1 Nephi 2

VERSE NUMBER

_____ a. Why did Lehi depart into the wilderness?

_____ b. In what year did Lehi and his family depart into the wilderness? (See p. 3, bottom right-hand corner.)

_____ c. When Lehi departed into the wilderness, what did he leave behind? What did he take with him?

_____ d. Why did Laman and Lemuel murmur against their father? (See also Bible Dictionary, p. 712, s.v. "Jerusalem.")

_____ e. What happened because of Nephi's "great desires to know of the mysteries of God"? (1 Nephi 2:16.)

_____ f. Upon what condition would Nephi be "a ruler and a teacher over [his] brethren"? (V. 22.)

---

1 Nephi 3

VERSE NUMBER

_____ a. When Lehi asked his sons to obtain the plates of brass from Laban, what did Nephi's brothers say? What did Nephi say?

_____ b. What did Nephi say to Laman and Lemuel when they were about to return to their father without the plates?

_____ c. What did Laban do when he saw Lehi's property? Why?

_____ d. What did the angel say to Laman and Lemuel?

_____ e. What did Laman and Lemuel do after the angel reproved them?

---

1 Nephi 4

_____ a. What did Laman and Lemuel do after Nephi spoke to them?

_____ b. How did Nephi know what to do when he returned for the plates?

_____ c. Why did Nephi slay Laban?

_____ d. What did Nephi think about when the Spirit said, "Slay him"? (1 Nephi 4:12.)

_____ e. Why did Laban's servant go with Nephi to the treasury?

_____ f. Why were Laman and Lemuel frightened when Nephi appeared?

_____ g. What did Zoram do that caused Nephi and his brothers not to worry about him?

---

1 Nephi 5

_____ a. What did Lehi say to Sariah to comfort her in their sons' absence?

_____ b. What did Lehi and his family do before he searched the plates of brass?

_____ c. List four things Lehi found when he searched the plates of brass. (See also Bible Dictionary, p. 678, s.v. "Genealogy"; p. 711, s.v. "Jeremiah"; p. 716, s.v. "Joseph.")

_____ d. What did Lehi prophesy concerning the plates of brass?

_____ e. Why were the records of great worth to Lehi and his family? (See also Mosiah 1:3–7.)

---

1 Nephi 6

_____ a. Who were Lehi and his family descended from? (See also 2 Nephi 3:4.)

_____ b. What was Nephi's intent in keeping this record?

_____ c. What kinds of things would Nephi's record contain?

---

1 Nephi 7

_____ a. Why did the Lord command Lehi to have his sons return to Jerusalem for Ishmael and his family?

_____ b. Why did Ishmael and his family depart into the wilderness?

_____ c. While they were returning to Lehi, Laman and Lemuel rebelled. What did Nephi say? What did Laman and Lemuel do? When Laman and Lemuel asked for forgiveness, what did Nephi do?

_____ d. What did Lehi do when his sons and Ishmael's family met him in the wilderness?

---

1 Nephi 8

_____ a. Why did Lehi, in his dream, rejoice for Nephi and Sam? fear for Laman and Lemuel?

_____ b. Many people started on the path that led to the tree of life. Why did many lose their way? How were the others able to reach the tree?

_____ c. What did Lehi do when he saw that Laman and Lemuel "partook not of the fruit"? (1 Nephi 8:35.)

---

1 Nephi 9

_____ a. Why did Nephi make these plates?

_____ b. What is recorded on the other plates?

---

1 Nephi 10

_____ a. What would happen six hundred years after Lehi left Jerusalem?

_____ b. Which verses tell about John the Baptist?

_____ c. Who was compared to an olive tree?

_____ d. What was Nephi's desire after he heard "all the words of [his] father"? (1 Nephi 10:17.)

_____ e. What will happen to those who diligently seek to know the things of God?

_____ f. For what will you be judged?

_____ g. Who gave Nephi authority to speak these words?

---

1 Nephi 11

_____ a. Why was Nephi able to "behold the things which [he] desired"? (1 Nephi 11:6.)

_____ b. Who is the virgin spoken of in verse 18? (See also v. 18a; Bible Dictionary, p. 729, "Mary.")

_____ c. Who is the child spoken of in 1 Nephi 11:20? (See also v. 20a.)

_____ d. What is the meaning of the tree that Nephi saw? (See also 1 Nephi 15:21–22.)

_____ e. What is the meaning of the rod of iron that Nephi saw? (See also 1 Nephi 15:23–24.)

_____ f. Why was the Savior lifted upon the cross and slain?

_____ g. What was the great and spacious building?

---

1 Nephi 12

_____ a. In which verse did Nephi describe the Savior's visit to his descendants?

_____ b. What was the mist of darkness that prevented many from reaching the tree of life?

_____ c. What do the temptations of the devil do to "the children of men"? (1 Nephi 12:17.)

_____ d. What was the large and spacious building that Lehi saw?

_____ e. Why would the Lamanites be able to overpower the Nephites after the visit of Jesus?

---

1 Nephi 13

_____ a. Who is the founder of the great and abominable church?

_____ b. In which verse does Nephi describe Christopher Columbus? the Pilgrims and other early pioneers? the Revolutionary War?

_____ c. What has the great and abominable church done to the Bible?

_____ d. What happened to many because the plain and precious things were taken from the Bible?

_____ e. What book, containing much of the gospel, was to come to the Gentiles?

---

1 Nephi 14

_____ a. What will happen to the Gentiles if they "hearken unto the Lamb of God" (1 Nephi 14:1) and "harden not their hearts" (v. 2)?

_____ b. What is the purpose of the great and abominable church?

_____ c. Which verse mentions the restoration of the gospel? (See also v. 7*a*.)

_____ d. In the last days, there will be only two churches. How big is the great and abominable church? How big is the church of the Lamb of God? Why?

_____ e. What would the Saints of God be armed with in the last days?

_____ f. Which apostle was ordained to record the things that Nephi had seen and would see? (See also v. 25*a* ; Revelation 1:9, 19.)

---

1 Nephi 15

VERSE NUMBER

_____ a. Why did Nephi's brothers argue about the things that Lehi saw?

_____ b. Why did Nephi consider his "afflictions were great above all"? (1 Nephi 15:5.)

_____ c. What question did Nephi ask his brothers when they could not understand the words of their father?

_____ d. In whose "seed shall all the kindreds of the earth be blessed"? (V. 18; see also Bible Dictionary, p. 602, s. v. "Abraham, Covenant of."

_____ e. Why is it important to hold fast to the iron rod?

_____ f. How hard did Nephi try to have his brothers keep the commandments?

_____ g. Why will the filthy be separated from the righteous in the day of judgment?

---

1 Nephi 16

VERSE NUMBER

_____ a. Why do "the guilty [take] the truth to be hard"? (1 Nephi 16:2.)

_____ b. What was the attitude of Nephi's brothers after he encouraged them to keep the commandments?

_____ c. What was the name of the ball that Lehi found at his tent door? (See v. 10*a*, Alma 37:38.)

_____ d. What happened in the group when Nephi broke his bow?

_____ e. How was Nephi able to find and "slay wild beasts" for food? (1 Nephi 16:31.)

_____ f. How did the pointers in the ball work?

_____ g. Who spoke to Laman and those he had stirred up to anger and caused them to repent?

1 Nephi 17

VERSE NUMBER

_____ a. How did the Lord bless Lehi's group?

_____ b. How will the Lord help us when we keep his commandments?

_____ c. For how many years did the group live in the wilderness?

_____ d. Why did they call the land Bountiful?

_____ e. What did Nephi say to the Lord when He asked him to build a ship?

_____ f. Why did Nephi's brothers murmur when he began to build a ship?

_____ g. Which people are favored of God?

_____ h. Why did the Lord speak to Nephi's brothers with a voice of thunder?

_____ i. What did Nephi say to his brothers when they came to kill him?

_____ j. How did Nephi's brothers know the Lord was with Nephi?

1 Nephi 18

VERSE NUMBER

_____ a. Why did the Lord show Nephi great things?

_____ b. What did Nephi's brothers and the sons of Ishmael and their wives do to make Nephi "fear exceedingly"? (1 Nephi 18:10.)

_____ c. What did Laman and Lemuel do after Nephi warned them to repent?

_____ d. What was the only thing that would soften the hearts of Nephi's brothers?

_____ e. How was Nephi freed from the bonds that held him?

_____ f. What did Lehi and his family "find upon the land of promise"? (V. 25.)

---

1 Nephi 19

_____ a. What did the Lord command Nephi to do when he arrived at the promised land?

_____ b. What were the people to do with the plates after Nephi died?

_____ c. What were the only things that Nephi wrote upon the plates?

_____ d. After how many years from the time Lehi left Jerusalem would Jesus be born?

_____ e. Why would the Lord suffer being smitten by the world?

_____ f. What would happen to the Jews at Jerusalem who crucified their God?

_____ g. Why did Nephi include the words of Isaiah in his record? (See also 1 Nephi 19:23d; Bible Dictionary, p. 707, s.v. "Isaiah.")

_____ h. Why should we "liken all scriptures unto us"? (1 Nephi 19:23.)

---

1 Nephi 20

_____ a. What does the Lord reveal to Israel?

_____ b. Who is to go forth from Babylon?

---

1 Nephi 21

_____ a. Who will be a light to the Gentiles?

_____ b. Who will be gathered with power in the last days?

_____ c. Who will help Israel in the last days?

---

1 Nephi 22

_____ a. How are things made known to the prophets?

_____ b. What is to happen to the house of Israel? (See also Bible Dictionary, p. 708, s.v. "Israel, Kingdom of.")

_____ c. Which verse describes the establishment of the United States? the restoration of the gospel?

_____ d. How are the righteous to be saved?

_____ e. Describe the churches "who need fear, and tremble, and quake." (1 Nephi 22:23.)

_____ f. Why will Satan have no power over the people for many years?

2 NEPHI

---

2 Nephi 1

_____ a. What had Lehi seen in his vision about Jerusalem?

_____ b. What did the Lord covenant with Lehi concerning the land of promise?

_____ c. Because the promised land is a land of liberty, what is the only thing that will bring into captivity the people who live there?

_____ d. Which verse speaks of those who settled America and fought the descendents of Lehi? (See also 2 Nephi 1:11a.)

_____ e. Why had Lehi's heart "been weighed down with sorrow from time to time"? (V. 17.)

_____ f. What did Lehi desire his sons to do so that his "soul might have joy" in them? (V. 21.)

_____ g. What blessing did Lehi give Zoram because of his faithfulness?

2 Nephi 2

VERSE NUMBER

_____ a. Why had Jacob "suffered afflictions and much sorrow"? (2 Nephi 2:1.)

_____ b. In which verse did Lehi record that Jacob had seen the Lord?

_____ c. For whom did Christ offer himself as a sacrifice for sin?

_____ d. What does there need to be in all the things that we do?

_____ e. What two types of things has God created?

_____ f. What needs to exist for us to act for ourselves? (See also v. 16b.)

_____ g. Why did Adam partake of the forbidden fruit? (See also Bible Dictionary, p. 670, s.v. "Fall of Adam.")

_____ h. How will we be acted upon?

_____ i. What are we free to choose while in the flesh?

_____ j. What is the "will of his Holy Spirit"? (2 Nephi 2:28.)

_____ k. What is the "will of the flesh and the evil which is therein"? (V. 29.)

_____ l. What was Lehi's only purpose in speaking to his sons?

2 Nephi 3

VERSE NUMBER

_____ a. Which verse describes the Lord's promise to Joseph who was sold into Egypt that a righteous branch of his descendants (Lehi's group) would be broken off (taken to a new land) and remembered of the Lord?

_____ b. Who is the seer mentioned in 2 Nephi 2:6–11? (See 7a.)

_____ c. What are the two records spoken of in verse 12 that will be used together in the last days? (See v. 12a, b.) What is their purpose?

_____ d. In which verse did Joseph reveal the name of the great seer of the last days?

_____ e. In which verse did Joseph reveal that the Book of Mormon would be translated and given to Lehi's descendants?

_____ f. Who is the person mentioned in verse 24? (See v. 24a.)

---

2 Nephi 4

VERSE NUMBER

_____ a. What did Nephi tell us was written on the plates of brass?

_____ b. What final blessing did Lehi leave with Laman's family? With Lemuel's family? With Sam?

_____ c. List seven things that Nephi recorded in 2 Nephi 4:20–25 to show that God supported him.

_____ d. What did Nephi ask the Lord to help him do "at the appearance of sin"? (V. 31.)

_____ e. Why did Nephi put his trust in God?

---

2 Nephi 5

VERSE NUMBER

_____ a. What did Nephi do "because of the anger of [his] brethren"? (2 Nephi 5:1.)

_____ b. How did Nephi know when to leave his brethren?

_____ c. What did the people of Nephi do to cause the Lord to bless them to "prosper exceedingly"? (V. 11.)

_____ d. How did the people of Nephi "prosper exceedingly"? (V. 11.)

_____ e. Nephi built a temple "after the manner of the temple" of whom? (V. 16; see also Bible Dictionary, p. 782, s.v. "Temple of Solomon.")

_____ f. Why did the Lord "cause a skin of blackness to come upon [Nephi's brethren]"? (2 Nephi 5:21.)

_____ g. What is one reason the Lord did not destroy Laman and Lemuel?

---

2 Nephi 6

VERSE NUMBER

_____ a. Why did Jacob speak to the people of Nephi?

_____ b. Which verse speaks of the earthly ministry of Christ to the Jews at Jerusalem?

_____ c. How will the Messiah "manifest himself unto [his people] in power and great glory" (2 Nephi 6:14.)?

_____ d. How will those who do not believe in the Messiah be destroyed?

---

2 Nephi 7

VERSE NUMBER

_____ a. Who will have the tongue of the learned?

_____ b. Who will not be confounded?

---

2 Nephi 8

VERSE NUMBER

_____ a. Who will the Lord gather in the last days?

_____ b. Who will come to Zion?

---

2 Nephi 9

VERSE NUMBER

_____ a. Why did Jacob read the words of Isaiah to the people?

_____ b. Why did Christ allow himself "to become subject unto man in the flesh, and die for all men"? (2 Nephi 9:5.)

_____ c. What would have happened to us if Christ had not made an infinite atonement? (See also Bible Dictionary, p. 617, s.v. "Atonement.")

_____ d. What would happen to our spirits "if the flesh should rise no more"? (2 Nephi 9:8.)

_____ e. What is another name for "the death of the spirit" (v. 10), or "the spiritual death" (v. 12)? (See also Bible Dictionary, p. 655, s.v. "Death"; p. 699, s.v. "Hell.")

_____ f. What will be restored "by the power of resurrection"? (2 Nephi 9:12.)

_____ g. What will you "have a perfect knowledge" of as a resurrected being? (V. 14.)

_____ h. What will happen to the filthy when they appear before the judgment seat of God? to the righteous?

_____ i. What will happen to those who did not know of God's laws?

_____ j. What will be the state of those who knew the laws of God and did not obey them?

_____ k. Why will many who are learned perish?

_____ l. Why will many "who are rich as to the things of the world" also perish? (V. 30.)

_____ m. What is the fate of those who tell lies? (See also v. 34a; Proverbs 19:9.)

_____ n. What kind of thoughts spoken of in 2 Nephi 9:39 should we have?

_____ o. What will the wicked "be constrained to exclaim" on the Day of Judgment? (V. 46.)

---

2 Nephi 10

VERSE NUMBER

_____ a. What did Jacob learn from the angel the previous night? (See also Bible Dictionary, p. 633, s.v. "Christ.")

_____ b. Why did Jesus come among the Jews?

_____ c. What would have happened if Jesus had performed his miracles among other nations?

_____ d. Why would the Jews at Jerusalem crucify him? (See also 2 Nephi 26:29; Bible Dictionary, p. 651, s.v. "Crucifixion.")

_____ e. Who is "the whore of the earth"? (2 Nephi 10:16.)

_____ f. Which verses mention other groups that God has led away from wickedness and destruction?

_____ g. What are we free to do?

_____ h. What does Jacob encourage us to reconcile ourselves to?

---

2 Nephi 11

_____ a. List the three people who Nephi told us had seen Jesus.

_____ b. List three things that Nephi's soul delighted in.

---

2 Nephi 12

_____ a. List three things Isaiah saw.

_____ b. What will happen to the proud and the wicked at the Second Coming of the Lord?

---

2 Nephi 13

_____ a. Who will be punished for their disobedience?

b. What will happen to the daughters of Zion because of their worldliness?

---

2 Nephi 14

_____ a. What will happen to "Zion and her daughters . . . in the millennial day"? (Headnote to 2 Nephi 14.)

---

2 Nephi 15

_____ a. What will happen to the Lord's vineyard (the house of Israel)?

_____ b. What will happen to them "in their apostate and scattered state"?

_____ c. What will the Lord do for the house of Israel in the last days?

---

2 Nephi 16

_____ a. Who did Isaiah see?

_____ b. What was Isaiah called to do?

_____ c. What did Isaiah prophesy of?

---

2 Nephi 17

_____ a. Who would wage war against Judah (the Jews)?

_____ b. Who would be "born of a virgin"?

---

2 Nephi 18

_____ a. What should we turn to for guidance?

---

2 Nephi 19

_____ a. Unto whom was a child to be born?

_____ b. What would that child do?

---

2 Nephi 20

_____ a. What is the destruction of Assyria a type of at the Second Coming?

_____ b. How many will be left after the Lord's second coming?

---

2 Nephi 21

_____ a. Who will judge in righteousness?

_____ b. What will cover the earth in the Millennium?

_____ c. How will the Lord gather Israel?

---

2 Nephi 22

_____ a. What will all people do in the millennial day?

_____ b. Who shall dwell among the people?

---

2 Nephi 23

_____ a. What will the Second Coming be a day of?

_____ b. What will happen to the wicked in the world?

---

2 Nephi 24

_____ a. What will happen to Israel?

_____ b. Why was Lucifer cast out of heaven? (See also Bible Dictionary, p. 726, s.v. "Lucifer.")

_____ c. Who will Israel triumph over?

---

2 Nephi 25

_____ a. To whom was Nephi writing? Why?

_____ b. What has the Lord always done before destroying any generation of the Jews?

_____ c. What happened to the Jews whom Nephi left in Jerusalem? Why?

_____ d. List three reasons Nephi gave for the Jews' rejecting Christ.

_____ e. After the Messiah has risen from the dead, what will happen to Jerusalem? to the Jews?

_____ f. When will the Lord "restore his people from their lost and fallen state"? (2 Nephi 25:17.)

_____ g. Who will come before the true Messiah and deceive the people?

_____ h. How many years after the time Nephi left Jerusalem would Jesus come to the Jews?

_____ i. What is the only "name given under heaven . . . whereby man can be saved"? (V. 20.)

_____ j. What did Nephi and his brethren "labor diligently" to do? (V. 23.) Why? (See also Bible Dictionary, p. 697, s.v. "Grace.")

_____ k. Why did Nephi "talk of Christ, . . . rejoice in Christ, . . . preach of Christ, . . . prophesy of Christ, and . . . write according to [the] prophecies"?

_____ l. What do we need to do to prevent our being cast out?

---

2 Nephi 26

_____ a. What would Christ do after being resurrected?

_____ b. How would the people of Nephi know of Christ's birth, death, and resurrection?

_____ c. What happens to those who "kill the prophets, and the saints"? (2 Nephi 26:5.)

_____ d. Why did Nephi experience so much pain and anguish in his soul?

_____ e. What would happen five generations from the time of Christ's visit to the righteous Nephites?

_____ f. What happens when the Spirit of the Lord ceases to strive with man?

_____ g. Which verse speaks of the coming forth of the Book of Mormon from out of the ground?

_____ h. Why do the Gentiles in our day "put down the power and miracles of God, and preach . . . their own wisdom and their own learning"? (V. 20.)

_____ i. What is the devil the founder of?

_____ j. How do you know that Christ loves the world?

_____ k. What is priestcraft?

_____ l. What will happen to the laborer in Zion who labors for money?

---

2 Nephi 27

VERSE NUMBER

_____ a. What will the Lord do to those nations who are "drunken with iniquity and all manner of abominations"? (2 Nephi 27:1.)

_____ b. What is recorded on the sealed portion of the plates, which Joseph Smith did not read? (See also v. 22.)

_____ c. By what power will "the words of the book which were sealed . . . be read upon the house tops"? (V. 11.)

_____ d. How many people are to bear testimony of the gold plates?

_____ e. Who is the one who is "learned" spoken of in verses 15–18? (See Joseph Smith–History 1:64–65.)

_____ f. What was Joseph Smith to do when he had finished translating the book?

_____ g. Who do those people follow who are mentioned in 2 Nephi 26:27? (See v. 22.)

2 Nephi 28

VERSE NUMBER

_____ a. For whom will the Book of Mormon "be of great worth"? (2 Nephi 28:2.)

_____ b. List four characteristics of the churches in the last days.

_____ c. What is wrong with the idea of "eat, drink, and be merry" as described in verses 7–8? (See Alma 34:32–34.)

_____ d. How have the churches in our day become corrupted?

_____ e. How have these churches robbed the poor?

_____ f. Who have not gone astray in our day?

_____ g. Why do the humble followers of Christ err in many instances?

_____ h. On whom has the Lord pronounced a triple "Wo"? (2 Nephi 28:15.)

_____ i. Why will the Lord shake the kingdom of the devil?

_____ j. List three methods the devil uses to capture the souls of men.

_____ k. How does the Lord give knowledge to the children of men?

2 Nephi 29

VERSE NUMBER

_____ a. From whom did we obtain the Bible? (See also Bible Dictionary, p. 622, s.v. "Bible"; Bible Dictionary, p. 713, s.v. "Jew.")

_____ b. How have the Gentiles treated the Jews?

_____ c. What does the Lord command all men to write? Why?

_____ d. What record did the Lord cause to be written that we do not yet have?

---

2 Nephi 30

_____ a. With whom does the Lord make covenants?

_____ b. How would the descendants of Lehi obtain the Book of Mormon?

_____ c. Why would they rejoice?

_____ d. What will the Jews do who are scattered throughout the world?

_____ e. What "great division" would the Lord soon make among the people of the earth?

_____ f. What knowledge will the righteous have in the Millennium?

---

2 Nephi 31

_____ a. Why was the Lord baptized? (See also Bible Dictionary, p. 618, s.v. "Baptism.")

_____ b. List six things required of us to "speak with the tongue of angels." (2 Nephi 31:13.)

_____ c. What did the Father say to Nephi?

_____ d. Why was Nephi shown the things that the Lord would do?

_____ e. What is "the gate by which [we] should enter"? (V. 17.)

_____ f. List five things from verse 20 that we must do to "have eternal life" after getting on the straight and narrow path. (V. 20.)

---

2 Nephi 32

_____ a. By what power do angels speak?

_____ b. Why must we "feast upon the words of Christ"? (2 Nephi 32:3.)

_____ c. Why is it important for us to obtain and listen to the Holy Ghost?

_____ d. Why was Nephi "left to mourn"? (V. 7.)

_____ e. What do you know when you "hearken unto the Spirit which teacheth a man to pray"? (V. 8.)

_____ f. Which spirit teaches a person "that he must not pray"? (V. 8.)

_____ g. Why should we "not perform any thing unto the Lord" without prayer? (V. 9; see also Bible Dictionary, p. 752, s.v. "Prayer.")

---

2 Nephi 33

_____ a. When is there great power in speaking?

_____ b. How do we know that Nephi had a great love for his people?

_____ c. List five reasons the words of Nephi would "be made strong" to his people. (2 Nephi 33:4.)

_____ d. Who would be angry with the words of Nephi?

_____ e. How will you know that Nephi recorded the words of Christ?

_____ f. What did Nephi say to those who will not believe the words of Christ?

JACOB

Jacob 1

_____ a. How many years after Lehi left Jerusalem was Jacob 1 written?

_____ b. How did the people know "of Christ and his kingdom, which should come"? (V. 6.)

_____ c. Why did Jacob and his brothers labor diligently among their people?

_____ d. Why did the people love Nephi?

_____ e. Who were called Lamanites?

_____ f. Who were called Nephites?

_____ g. How did Jacob and Joseph "magnify [their] office unto the Lord"? (V. 19.)

Jacob 2

_____ a. How did Jacob know that the people were beginning "to labor in sin"? (Jacob 2:5.)

_____ b. How did Jacob know that he was to go to the temple to declare the word of God?

_____ c. What did they do who obtained more riches than their brethren?

_____ d. What would happen if the rich persisted in their pride?

_____ e. What should we seek before riches?

_____ f. What should be the purpose of those who seek riches?

_____ g. How many wives were the Nephite men to have?

Jacob 3

_____ a. What did Jacob say to the "pure in heart" who have difficulties? (Jacob 3:1.)

_____ b. What would the Lord do if the wicked did not repent? (See also v. 4a; Omni 1:12–13.)

_____ c. Why were the Lamanites more righteous than the Nephites? (See also Jacob 2:35.)

_____ d. What was the unbelief and hatred of the Lamanites a result of?

Jacob 4

_____ a. Why did Jacob write on the plates only a little of his speaking?

_____ b. What was the intent of Jacob in writing upon the plates?

_____ c. Why should we not despise the revelations of God?

_____ d. Why should we seek counsel from the Lord?

_____ e. Why did God give the Jews "many things which they cannot understand"? (Jacob 4:14.)

Jacob 5

_____ a. What do the two olive trees represent?

_____ b. Who wrote the allegory of the tame and the wild olive trees?

_____ c. Why did Jacob record the allegory of the tame and the wild olive trees? (See Jacob 4:15–18.)

Jacob 6

_____ a. Which verse speaks of the reward of being a good missionary?

_____ b. What did Jacob beseech of his brethren "in words of soberness" to do? (Jacob 6:5.)

_____ c. What will happen to those who reject Christ and his plan?

_____ d. What counsel did Jacob give in verse 12? Why?

Jacob 7

_____ a. What did Sherem teach the people? Why?

_____ b. What could Sherem do because he was learned?

_____ c. Why was Sherem unable to shake Jacob?

_____ d. How was Jacob able to confound Sherem, even though Sherem had great power of speech?

_____ e. What sign was given to Sherem of the power of Christ?

_____ f. What did Sherem tell the people before he died?

_____ g. What did the multitude do as a result of Sherem's confession?

_____ h. What did Jacob do when he was about to die?

ENOS

Enos 1

_____ a. Who was the father of Enos? (See Enos 1:1a.)

_____ b. Why did Enos kneel down before his maker?

_____ c. How long did Enos pray?

_____ d. What did the Lord say to Enos?

_____ e. How was the guilt of Enos swept away?

_____ f. What was Enos's first desire after he had been forgiven of his sins?

_____ g. What desire caused Enos to pray "with many long strugglings"? (V. 11.)

_____ h. What else did Enos "cry unto God" for? (V. 16.)

_____ i. What was the only thing that many of the Lamanites ate?

_____ j. Nothing short of what things would prevent the Nephites "from going down speedily to destruction"? (V. 23.)

JAROM

Jarom 1

_____ a. Who was the father of Jarom?

_____ b. Who had communion with the Holy Ghost?

_____ c. How were the Nephites able to withstand the Lamanites?

_____ d. With what penalty did the prophets "threaten the people of Nephi"? (Jarom 1:10.)

OMNI

Omni 1

_____ a. Who was the father of Omni?

_____ b. What did Omni do in his days?

_____ c. To whom did Omni deliver the plates?

_____ d. What happened in the days of Amaron?

_____ e. Whom did the Lord spare from destruction?

_____ f. To whom did Amaron deliver the plates?

_____ g. When did Amaron make his record on the plates?

_____ h. Who was the father of Abinadom?

_____ i. What did Abinadom see in his days?

_____ j. Who received the record after Abinadom?

_____ k. What did the Lord warn the righteous to do in the days of Mosiah?

_____ l. Who did Mosiah and the righteous discover when they were led from the land of Nephi to the land of Zarahemla? (See also Helaman 8:21.)

_____ m. Why did the people of Zarahemla deny Christ?

_____ n. Why did Amaleki deliver the plates to King Benjamin? (See also Words of Mormon 1:10.)

_____ o. Why were many of the group killed as they tried to return to the land of Nephi?

WORDS OF MORMON

Words of Mormon 1

VERSE NUMBER

_____ a. What was Mormon about to do?

_____ b. What was Mormon's prayer?

_____ c. How did King Benjamin fight the Lamanites?

_____ d. How were the Nephites able to drive the Lamanites out of their lands?

_____ e. How was King Benjamin able to establish peace in the land?

MOSIAH

Mosiah 1

_____ a. Who was the father of King Benjamin? (See Omni 1:23.)

_____ b. What did the Nephites have that prevented them from becoming like the Lamanites?

_____ c. Who did King Benjamin desire to bestow his kingdom upon?

_____ d. What name did King Benjamin desire to bestow upon his people? Why? (See Mosiah 5:8.)

_____ e. List five things King Benjamin gave to Mosiah.

Mosiah 2

_____ a. List four reasons why the people wanted to thank God.

_____ b. Why was the tower built?

_____ c. How did King Benjamin begin his speech to the people?

_____ d. Why did King Benjamin relate a brief history of his reign in Mosiah 2:11–14?

_____ e. Whose service was King Benjamin in when he served his people faithfully?

_____ f. Whose service are we in when we help our family, friends, and neighbors?

_____ g. What would we be if we thanked God and served Him with our whole soul?

_____ h. What does the Lord require for us to "prosper in the land"? (V. 22.)

_____ i. What did the Lord command King Benjamin to declare unto the people?

_____ j. What did King Benjamin specifically warn his people to beware of?

_____ k. What is the fate of those who do contrary to what they know to be right and do not repent?

_____ l. What is the state of those who keep the commandments?

Mosiah 3

_____ a. Why did the angel appear to King Benjamin?

_____ b. What things would the Lord suffer during his earthly ministry?

_____ c. For whose sins does the blood of Christ atone?

_____ d. What is the only name, way, or means to gain salvation?

_____ e. What must the natural man do in order *not* to be an enemy to God?

_____ f. What is the fate of those whose works have been evil?

Mosiah 4

_____ a. Why had the multitude "fallen to the earth"? (Mosiah 4:1.)

_____ b. What happened when the people cried for forgiveness of their sins?

_____ c. How were the people able to obtain a "peace of conscience"? (V. 3.)

_____ d. What must you do if you believe King Benjamin's words?

_____ e. What counsel did King Benjamin give in verse 11?

_____ f. List ten reasons for following this counsel.

_____ g. What did King Benjamin say to those who would deny the beggar and say, "The man has brought upon himself his misery"? (V. 17.)

_____ h. What should the poor say in their hearts to the beggar?

_____ i. How do we retain "a remission of [our] sins from day to day, that [we] may walk guiltless before God"? (V. 26.)

_____ j. Why should we not try to do more than we have strength for?

_____ k. What should we do with those things that we borrow?

_____ l. What do we need to watch so that we will not perish?

Mosiah 5

_____ a. What mighty change did the Spirit of the Lord perform in the hearts of the people?

_____ b. What brought the people to the great knowledge described in Mosiah 5:3?

_____ c. What did the people covenant with the Lord? (See also Bible Dictionary, p. 651, s.v. "Covenant.")

_____ d. Why were the people called "the children of Christ"? (Mosiah 5:7.)

_____ e. What will cause the name of Christ to be "blotted out of [our] hearts"? (V. 11.)

_____ f. Why is it important to hear and know "the name by which ye are called"? (V. 14.)

_____ g. What must you do for Christ to "seal you his"? (V. 15.)

Mosiah 6

_____ a. Who did not covenant to take upon themselves the name of Christ?

_____ b. What did King Benjamin appoint priests to do?

_____ c. List five things King Mosiah did as king.

Mosiah 7

_____ a. Who did King Mosiah desire to know about? (See Omni 1:12, 27–30.)

_____ b. Where did the people spoken of in Omni 1:27–30 want to live? (See also v. 27c.)

_____ c. Who led the group that went to the land of Lehi-Nephi?

_____ d. Why was King Limhi "exceedingly glad" after Ammon had spoken? (Mosiah 7:14.)

_____ e. What was the relationship of King Limhi and his people to the Lamanites?

_____ f. Why did the Lamanites yield the cities of Lehi-Nephi and Shilom to Zeniff and his group?

_____ g. How much tribute did King Limhi's people pay to the Lamanites?

_____ h. Why did the Lord allow them to be brought into bondage?

_____ i. Who was the prophet of the Lord that they had slain? (See v. 26a.)

_____ j. What did the people need to do to be delivered "out of bondage"? (V. 33.)

Mosiah 8

VERSE NUMBER

_____ a. Whose great speech did Ammon teach to King Limhi's people?

_____ b. What chapters contain the record of King Limhi's people from the time they left the land of Zarahemla? (See Mosiah 8:5a.)

_____ c. Why did King Limhi desire to have the twenty-four gold plates translated?

_____ d. Who was Ammon referring to in verse 13? (See Mosiah 28:17–19.)

_____ e. What book in the Book of Mormon was written on the twenty-four gold plates? (See Ether 1:2.)

_____ f. What is a seer? (See Mosiah 28:13–16; see also Bible Dictionary, p. 771, s.v. "Seer.")

Mosiah 9

VERSE NUMBER

_____ a. Whose record is contained in Mosiah 9 through 22?

_____ b. Why did the first group that returned to the land of Nephi fight among themselves? (See also Omni 1:27–30.)

_____ c. Why was the second group "smitten with famine and sore afflictions"? (Mosiah 9:3.)

_____ d. Why did the Lamanite king want to bring Zeniff and his people into bondage?

_____ e. How were Zeniff and his people able to drive the Lamanites out of their land?

Mosiah 10

VERSE NUMBER

_____ a. What did Zeniff do to protect his people from the Lamanites?

_____ b. Why did the Lamanites attack Zeniff and his people?

_____ c. Why did the Lamanites "have an eternal hatred towards the children of Nephi"? (Mosiah 10:17.)

_____ d. How were Zeniff and his people able to drive the Lamanites out of their land?

Mosiah 11

VERSE NUMBER

_____ a. Upon whom did Zeniff confer his kingdom?

_____ b. What did King Noah place his heart upon?

_____ c. How did King Noah spend his time?

_____ d. Who did the Lord send to warn the people to repent?

_____ e. What message did Abinadi deliver to the people?

_____ f. Why did King Noah want to kill Abinadi?

Mosiah 12

VERSE NUMBER

_____ a. What did the Lord command Abinadi to tell the people?

_____ b. Why would the Lord smite the people?

_____ c. How was Abinadi able to withstand the questions of King Noah's priests and to confound them in their words? (See Mosiah 12:19*b*.)

_____ d. How did the priests of King Noah pervert "the ways of the Lord"? (V. 26.)

_____ e. Why should the priests "tremble before God"? (V. 30.)

Mosiah 13

_____ a. What did Abinadi tell the priests would happen to them if they touched him? Why?

_____ b. How did the priests know the Spirit of the Lord was upon Abinadi?

_____ c. Why did Abinadi read "the remainder of the commandments of God" to King Noah and his priests? (Mosiah 13:11; see also Bible Dictionary, p. 648, s.v. "Commandments, the Ten.")

_____ d. Why was "a very strict law," the law of Moses, given to the children of Israel? (Mosiah 13:29.)

_____ e. The law of Moses was a law of what? (See also Bible Dictionary, p. 722, s.v. "Law of Moses.")

_____ f. Why did the children of Israel fail to understand the law of Moses?

Mosiah 14

_____ a. What did Isaiah prophesy of concerning Christ?

Mosiah 15

_____ a. Why is Jesus called the Son of God?

_____ b. Why is Jesus called the Father?

_____ c. Who will take part in the first resurrection?

_____ d. Who will not take part in the first resurrection?

Mosiah 16

VERSE NUMBER

_____ a. Abinadi told King Noah and his priests that the time would come when all people would see what and do what?

_____ b. Why will the wicked be cast out?

_____ c. What would have happened to all mankind if God had not redeemed his people? (See also Mosiah 15:19–20.)

_____ d. How is the devil able to obtain power over us?

_____ e. What is the fate of those whom the devil has power over?

_____ f. How will we be judged?

_____ g. Who will be resurrected to endless happiness? to endless damnation?

Mosiah 17

VERSE NUMBER

_____ a. What did King Noah command his priests to do with Abinadi?

_____ b. What caused King Noah to seek Alma's life?

_____ c. Who recorded the message that the Lord commanded Abinadi to deliver?

_____ d. What excuse did King Noah use to command that Abinadi be put to death?

_____ e. How could Abinadi have avoided being put to death?

_____ f. Why was King Noah about to release Abinadi?

Mosiah 18

_____ a. What did Alma teach many of the people privately?

_____ b. Where did Alma teach the people?

_____ c. What did the people desire who believed the words of Alma?

_____ d. What is the covenant we made at the time of our baptism?

_____ e. How were the priests to be rewarded for their work in the ministry? Why?

_____ f. How were the members of the Church to use their riches?

_____ g. Upon being discovered by the king, what did Alma and his group do?

_____ h. How many people were in Alma's group?

Mosiah 19

_____ a. Why did Gideon spare the life of King Noah?

_____ b. What did King Noah command all the men to do when the Lamanites began to overtake his people?

_____ c. Why did the Lamanites refrain from killing those who remained?

_____ d. Who was Limhi?

_____ e. What happened to King Noah? (See also Mosiah 17:18.)

_____ f. What oath did the king of the Lamanites make with Limhi?

_____ g. What oath did Limhi make with the king of the Lamanites?

Mosiah 20

_____ a. Why did the priests of King Noah fail to return to the city of Nephi?

_____ b. What did these priests do that made the Lamanites angry?

_____ c. How were Limhi and his people able to defeat the Lamanites?

_____ d. Why did the Lamanite army refrain from destroying Limhi's people when they returned?

Mosiah 21

_____ a. Why did the Lamanites dare not kill any of the Nephites?

_____ b. Why did the Nephites go to battle against the Lamanites?

_____ c. What did the Nephites do after losing three battles with the Lamanites?

_____ d. How did the Lord help the Nephites?

_____ e. Why did the Nephites desire to capture the priests of King Noah?

_____ f. Why were Ammon and his brethren thrown into prison? (See also Mosiah 21:21a.)

_____ g. Why were King Limhi and his people unable to be baptized?

_____ h. What did Ammon, King Limhi, and all the people study to do?

Mosiah 22

_____ a. Why did the Nephites decide to escape into the wilderness?

_____ b. What plan of escape did Gideon present to King Limhi?

_____ c. How did the Nephites escape from the Lamanites?

_____ d. How did Mosiah receive King Limhi and his people?

_____ e. What happened to the Lamanite army that was sent after the Nephites?

Mosiah 23

_____ a. Whose story is recorded in Mosiah 23 and 24? (See also Mosiah 23:1a.)

_____ b. How were Alma and his people able to escape from King Noah?

_____ c. Why did Alma discourage the people from having a king?

_____ d. What kind of people should teachers and ministers be?

_____ e. From whom did the preachers and teachers in the Church in Alma's day receive their authority?

_____ f. What did the Nephites do when the Lamanite army came?

_____ g. Why did the Lamanite army refrain from killing the priests of King Noah?

_____ h. What promise did the Lamanites make and then break with Alma?

Mosiah 24

_____ a. What did Amulon and his brethren teach the Lamanites?

_____ b. What did Amulon and his brethren not teach the Lamanites?

_____ c. What was the result?

_____ d. What penalty did Amulon decree for those Nephites who prayed?

_____ e. How did the Lord ease the burdens of the Nephites?

_____ f. How were Alma and his people able to escape?

_____ g. What did the people do in the valley of Alma?

_____ h. How did King Mosiah receive Alma and his people?

Mosiah 25

_____ a. Who were the Mulekites? (See Omni 1:14–19.)

_____ b. Which records did King Mosiah read to the people?

_____ c. How did the Nephites feel toward the Lamanites?

_____ d. Why were all the people of Zarahemla called Nephites?

_____ e. What did King Limhi and his people desire to do after Alma had spoken to them?

_____ f. What power did King Mosiah grant to Alma?

_____ g. What happened to those who took upon themselves the name of Christ?

Mosiah 26

_____ a. Why did many of the Nephites harden their hearts?

_____ b. Why did they remain a separate people "even in their carnal and sinful state"? (Mosiah 26:4.)

_____ c. Why was Alma "troubled in his spirit"? (V. 10.)

_____ d. What happens to those who sin, if they confess and repent with sincerity of heart? if they do not repent?

_____ e. What did Alma and his fellow laborers do that caused the Church to prosper exceedingly?

Mosiah 27

_____ a. What laws did the Nephites obey to become "a large and wealthy people"? (Mosiah 27:7.)

_____ b. Who were among the nonbelievers?

_____ c. What were they doing when the angel appeared and spoke to them?

_____ d. Why did the angel come to convince them "of the power and authority of God"? (V. 14.)

_____ e. Why did Alma and the priests fast and pray?

_____ f. What message did Alma the Younger give after he received his strength?

_____ g. What did Alma do from that time forward?

Mosiah 28

_____ a. What was the desire of the sons of King Mosiah?

_____ b. To whom did King Mosiah take their request?

_____ c. What did the Lord say to King Mosiah?

_____ d. Who is called a seer?

_____ e. Where is the translation of the twenty-four gold plates found? (See Ether 1:2.)

_____ f. To whom did King Mosiah give the plates?

Mosiah 29

_____ a. What kind of men did King Mosiah recommend be appointed as judges?

_____ b. Why did King Mosiah recommend that the people not have a king?

_____ c. How is a wicked king dethroned?

_____ d. Why should the business of governing be done by the voice of the people?

_____ e. With respect to government, when will the judgments of God come upon the people?

_____ f. What did King Mosiah desire of the people?

_____ g. What did King Mosiah do in Mosiah 29:33–38 before the people voted for their new judges?

_____ h. Why did the people rejoice?

_____ i. How did the people feel toward King Mosiah?

_____ j. Who was the first chief judge?

_____ k. How many years before the coming of Christ did Alma and King Mosiah die?

ALMA

Alma 1

_____ a. List three things that Nehor taught the people.

_____ b. What is priestcraft? (See 2 Nephi 26:29.))

_____ c. Why did many embrace priestcraft and teach false doctrine?

_____ d. Why did these people dare not lie, steal, rob, or murder?

_____ e. Why were the members of the Church persecuted?

_____ f. How were the members of the Church to treat nonmembers and other Church members?

_____ g. What happened to those Church members who hardened their hearts?

46

_____ h. How did the members of the Church treat the poor and the needy?

_____ i. Why did the Church members become more wealthy than the nonmembers?

Alma 2

_____ a. What would Amlici have done to the church of God if he had been made king?

_____ b. How were the Nephites able to beat the Amlicites in the first battle?

_____ c. Why did the spies whom Alma had sent to watch the Amlicites return quickly, being "struck with much fear"? (Alma 2:23.)

_____ d. How were the Nephites able to beat the Amlicites in the second battle?

_____ e. Why was Alma not killed by Amlici?

_____ f. What happened to many of the Amlicites and Lamanites in the wilderness?

Alma 3

_____ a. What was the difference in appearance between a Lamanite and an Amlicite?

_____ b. Why did the Lamanites have a dark skin?

_____ c. Why did Alma not go with the Nephites to battle the Lamanites?

_____ d. What happened to those Nephites, Lamanites, and Amlicites who died in battle in the fifth year of the reign of judges?

Alma 4

_____ a. How great was the affliction of the Nephites because of their battles with the Lamanites and Amlicites?

_____ b. What did their mourning cause the people to do?

_____ c. What was "the cause of much affliction to Alma"? (Alma 4:7.)

_____ d. What effect did the actions of the Church members have on the nonmembers?

_____ e. What were the humble followers of God doing?

_____ f. Why did Alma give up the judgment seat?

Alma 5

VERSE NUMBER

_____ a. Where did Alma begin "to deliver the word of God"? (Alma 5:1.)

_____ b. How were Alma and his people saved from death and hell, as spoken of in verse 10?

_____ c. What is your answer to Alma's questions in verses 14 through 35?

_____ d. Who is the shepherd of those who "will not hearken unto the voice of the good shepherd"? (V. 38.)

_____ e. How do you know who follows the Good Shepherd?

_____ f. How did Alma know these things were true?

_____ g. List six reasons given in verses 53 through 56 why the people were under condemnation.

h. What did Alma command the members of the Church to do?

Alma 6

_____ a. After Alma's speech to the people in Zarahemla, what happened to those nonmembers who repented? to those Church members who did not repent?

_____ b. What were the Church members commanded to do often? Why?

_____ c. Where did Alma go after he had taught the people in the city of Zarahemla?

Alma 7

_____ a. What was the reason for Alma's "exceedingly great joy"? (Alma 7:4.)

_____ b. What was the most important thing of all the things to come?

_____ c. What had the Spirit told Alma?

_____ d. What is required of us to enter the kingdom of heaven?

_____ e. What does it mean to be "born again"? (V. 14.)

_____ f. Why did Alma say these things to the people?

_____ g. In verses 23 and 24, what did Alma say he wanted the people to do?

Alma 8

_____ a. Which people did Alma teach next?

_____ b. How did the people in the land of Melek receive Alma's message?

_____ c. Why would the people of Ammonihah "not hearken unto the words of Alma"? (Alma 8:9.)

_____ d. How did the people treat Alma?

_____ e. Why did the angel appear to Alma?

_____ f. How did the Lord prepare the way for Alma to return to the city?

_____ g. Why was Alma hungry when he met Amulek?

_____ h. What power did Alma and Amulek have when they went among the people?

Alma 9

_____ a. Who will you read about in Alma 9 through 14?

_____ b. What did Alma tell the people would happen if they did not repent?

_____ c. Why has the Lord been merciful to the Lamanites?

_____ d. List twelve ways in which the Nephites were highly favored of the Lord.

_____ e. How will we be rewarded?

_____ f. How did the people feel toward Alma? Why?

Alma 10

_____ a. How did Amulek know that Alma was a holy man?

_____ b. Who were the people who sought to destroy Alma and Amulek?

_____ c. What was the only thing preventing the destruction of the city of Ammonihah?

_____ d. How would they have been destroyed if they had cast out the righteous from among them?

_____ e. Who was the lawyer who "was the foremost to accuse Amulek and Alma"? (Alma 10:31.)

_____ f. What was the object of the lawyers?

Alma 11

VERSE NUMBER

_____ a. Why did the lawyers "stir up the people against Alma and Amulek"? (Alma 11:20.)

_____ b. Why will the Lord not save us in our sins?

_____ c. Whose transgressions will the Lord take upon himself?

_____ d. What is "temporal death"? (V. 42.)

_____ e. What will we remember when we stand before God?

_____ f. What did Zeezrom do when Amulek finished speaking?

Alma 12

VERSE NUMBER

_____ a. What did Zeezrom do after Alma spoke to him concerning his "lying and craftiness"? (Alma 12:3.) Why?

_____ b. How are we able to know the mysteries of God in full?

_____ c. What happens to those who harden their hearts?

_____ d. What is meant by the "chains of hell"? (V. 11.)

_____ e. What will condemn us when we stand before the judgment bar of God?

_____ f. What is "spiritual death" and who will suffer it? (See also Helaman 14:18; Alma 40:26; 42:9.)

_____ g. What are we to do while on this earth?

_____ h. What will happen to those who repent and do not harden their heart? to those who do not repent and do harden their heart?

Alma 13

_____ a. Why were priests ordained after the holy order of God?

_____ b. Who were ordained high priests?

_____ c. What happened to those who were "sanctified by the Holy Ghost"? (Alma 13:12.)

_____ d. Why was Melchizedek called the "prince of peace"? (V. 18.)

_____ e. Why were angels declaring repentance to many in other parts of the land?

_____ f. What did Alma wish from the "inmost part" of his heart? (V. 27.)

Alma 14

_____ a. What did the people do when Alma had finished speaking to them?

_____ b. What did Zeezrom do when Alma and Amulek were delivered up to the chief judge of the land?

_____ c. What did the people do to those men who believed in the word of God? to their wives and children? to the holy scriptures?

_____ d. Why does the Lord suffer the righteous to be slain by the wicked?

_____ e. How were Alma and Amulek treated by the people?

_____ f. How great was the fear of those who persecuted Alma and Amulek in prison?

_____ g. Why did the people outside the prison flee from Alma and Amulek?

Alma 15

_____ a. Who did Alma and Amulek meet in the land of Sidom?

_____ b. Why did Zeezrom lie sick with a burning fever?

_____ c. How was Zeezrom healed?

_____ d. What did Zeezrom do after his baptism?

_____ e. What did Amulek leave in the land of Ammonihah?

_____ f. What did Alma do for Amulek?

Alma 16

_____ a. What happened to the people who were in Ammonihah?

_____ b. How were Zoram and his armies able to take the Nephite captives from the Lamanite army?

_____ c. Why did the people stay out of the land of Ammonihah for many years?

_____ d. Why did the Lord "pour out his Spirit" upon the land? (Alma 16:16.)

_____ e. What did the people "hear with great joy and gladness"? (V. 20.)

Alma 17

_____ a. Whose account is recorded in Alma 17 through 26? (See also Mosiah 28:1, 7–9.)

_____ b. Why did Alma "rejoice exceedingly" when he met the sons of Mosiah? (Alma 17:2.)

_____ c. What did the sons of Mosiah do in order to teach "with power and authority of God"? (See also Bible Dictionary, p. 671, s.v. "Fasts.")

_____ d. How long had the sons of Mosiah been on their mission to the Lamanites?

_____ e. What kind of afflictions had they experienced?

_____ f. Why did the group members fast and pray while they traveled to the Lamanites?

_____ g. What happened to Ammon when he entered the land of Ishmael?

_____ h. Why were the servants of King Lamoni fearful when their flocks were scattered? (See also Alma 18:6.)

_____ i. Why was Ammon's heart filled with joy when he saw that the flocks had been scattered?

_____ j. What were presented "unto the king for a testimony of the things" that had been done? (Alma 17:39.)

Alma 18

VERSE NUMBER

_____ a. What did King Lamoni say after the servants testified of the things they had seen?

_____ b. Why did the Lamanites scatter the flocks of the king?

_____ c. Where was Ammon when King Lamoni wanted to speak with him?

_____ d. What did Ammon desire of King Lamoni?

_____ e. What did the king do after Ammon had taught him?

Alma 19

VERSE NUMBER

_____ a. What did the queen desire of Ammon?

_____ b. Why did Ammon bless the queen?

_____ c. When King Lamoni arose from his sleep, what did he say to his people?

_____ d. Who then fell to the earth?

_____ e. Who was Abish?

_____ f. Why did Abish want the people to come to the house of the king?

_____ g. What happened to the man who attempted to kill Ammon?

_____ h. What did the servants of King Lamoni declare unto the people?

_____ i. What did those people do who believed the words of King Lamoni and his servants?

Alma 20

VERSE NUMBER

_____ a. Why did Ammon not go with Lamoni to the land of Nephi?

_____ b. What did King Lamoni's father command Lamoni to do?

_____ c. What did Ammon say to King Lamoni's father to protect Lamoni?

_____ d. What two things did Ammon require of King Lamoni's father?

_____ e. What did King Lamoni's father request of Ammon?

Alma 21

VERSE NUMBER

_____ a. Whose account is recorded in Alma 21 through 26?

_____ b. Who were the people of Amulon? (See Mosiah 23:31–32; 24:1, 4.)

_____ c. Who was Nehor? (See Alma 21:4b.)

_____ d. What did the people in the city of Jerusalem do when Aaron began to teach them of Christ?

_____ e. What happened to Aaron and some of his brethren in Middoni?

_____ f. How did Aaron and his brethren know where to preach?

_____ g. What freedom did King Lamoni declare unto the people in his kingdom?

Alma 22

_____ a. Where did the Spirit lead Aaron?

_____ b. Why was the king "troubled in mind"? (Alma 22:3.)

_____ c. What did the king want to know after he had been taught by Aaron?

_____ d. What was the king willing to give up in order to know the great joy that was spoken of by Aaron?

_____ e. What was the king's prayer?

_____ f. What was the king willing to give away in order to know God?

_____ g. How was the king's household converted to the Lord?

Alma 23

_____ a. What was the message of the king's proclamation?

_____ b. How many Lamanites "were brought to the knowledge of the Lord"? (Alma 23:5.)

_____ c. Which people hardened their hearts?

_____ d. By what name did those who were converted choose to call themselves?

_____ e. What did the converted Lamanites do?

Alma 24

_____ a. Who stirred up the Lamanites to anger and to make war upon their brethren?

_____ b. Why did the Anti-Nephi-Lehis bury their swords?

_____ c. Why were the Anti-Nephi-Lehis willing to suffer death rather than commit sin?

_____ d. Why did the Lamanites prepare for war?

_____ e. What did the Anti-Nephi-Lehis do when they saw the Lamanite army coming to slay them?

_____ f. Why did many Lamanites throw down their weapons?

_____ g. What groups of Lamanites slew the greatest number of their brethren?

_____ h. Why did the Amalekites and Amulonites have such hard hearts?

Alma 25

VERSE NUMBER

_____ a. Where did the armies of the Lamanites go next? (See also Alma 16:2–3.)

_____ b. What happened to many of the Amulonites in the war with the Nephites?

_____ c. What happened to those in the Lamanite army who were converted to the Lord in the wilderness?

_____ d. What did the Lamanites do to the seed of Amulon and his brethren?

_____ e. What did many of the Lamanite army do when they returned home?

_____ f. Why did the sons of Mosiah and their brethren "rejoice exceedingly"? (Alma 25:17.)

Alma 26

VERSE NUMBER

_____ a. What great blessing was bestowed upon Ammon and his brethren?

_____ b. What hope is there for those who have sinned? (See Alma 26:18–22.)

_____ c. Who "is given to know the mysteries of God"? (V. 22.)

_____ d. How should we treat our enemies?

_____ e. What did the Lord say to Ammon and his brethren when they were depressed and about to turn back?

_____ f. Why did they suffer "all manner of afflictions" during their ministry? (V. 30.)

Alma 27

VERSE NUMBER

_____ a. How were Ammon and his brethren treated by the people of Anti-Nephi-Lehi?

_____ b. What was the plan to save the Anti-Nephi-Lehis from being destroyed by the Lamanites?

_____ c. Upon what condition did the king consent to go to the land of Zarahemla?

_____ d. Who did Ammon and his brethren meet while they were on the way to talk with the Nephites?

_____ e. Where else in the book of Alma is this meeting recorded?

_____ f. Who are those who experience "exceeding joy"?

_____ g. What was the name of the place that the Nephites gave the people of Anti-Nephi-Lehi to live?

_____ h. Why did the people of Anti-Nephi-Lehi refuse to defend themselves against the Lamanites? (See also Helaman 15:9.)

_____ i. By what name did the Nephites call the people of Anti-Nephi-Lehi?

Alma 28

VERSE NUMBER

_____ a. How did the Nephites cope with their sorrow?

_____ b. Why did the Nephites mourn and rejoice at the same time?

_____ c. What makes men unequal?

Alma 29

_____ a. Why did Alma want to be an angel?

_____ b. What is given to those who know good and evil?

_____ c. What was Alma's glory?

_____ d. Why was Alma's joy "more full"? (Alma 29:14.)

Alma 30

_____ a. What was there no law against?

_____ b. Under Nephite law, for what actions would someone be punished?

_____ c. What was the name of the antichrist who began to preach to the people? (See also Bible Dictionary, p. 609, s.v. "Antichrist.")

_____ d. Why could the law "have no hold upon him"? (Alma 30:12.)

_____ e. What did Korihor teach the people?

_____ f. Why was Korihor brought before Alma and the chief judge?

_____ g. What evidence did Korihor have that Christ would not come?

_____ h. What evidence did Alma have that Christ would come?

_____ i. Why did Korihor deny that which he believed to be true?

_____ j. What sign was Korihor given that there is a God?

_____ k. What did Korihor write in response to the questions of the chief judge?

_____ l. Why was the curse not taken from Korihor?

_____ m. How does the devil take care of his people "at the last day"? (V. 60.)

Alma 31

_____ a. What caused great sorrow to Alma?

_____ b. What did the Nephites fear the Zoramites would do?

_____ c. What had a more powerful effect upon the people than anything else? (See also Alma 26:23–33.)

_____ d. What was the Rameumpton used for?

_____ e. Why was Alma's heart grieved? What were the hearts of the Zoramites "set upon"? (Alma 31:24.) What were their hearts "lifted up unto"? (V. 25.)

_____ f. What pained Alma's soul?

_____ g. What did those who were with Alma do after his prayer and after being filled with the Holy Ghost?

Alma 32

_____ a. Among which part of the Zoramites did the missionaries begin to have success?

_____ b. Why had these people been cast out of the synagogues?

_____ c. Why did Alma have great joy at seeing the multitude and hearing their concern?

_____ d. Why are those blessed who are compelled to be humble?

_____ e. Why is faith not obtained by having "a sign from heaven"? (Alma 32:17.)

_____ f. Why does God not perform miracles for those who have no faith? (See also Ether 12:6, 12, 18; Bible Dictionary, p. 732, s.v. "Miracles.")

_____ g. What is faith? (See also Bible Dictionary, p. 669, s.v. "Faith.")

_____ h. What is the first step in obtaining faith?

_____ i. To whom does God impart his word?

_____ j. What did Alma compare to a seed?

_____ k. Where are we to plant this seed?

_____ l. What will happen if the seed sprouts and the tree begins to grow but is then neglected?

_____ m. How will we be able to feast upon the fruit of the tree so that we will not hunger or thirst?

Alma 33

_____ a. List the five places where Zenos had prayed and the Lord had heard him.

_____ b. Why did Zenos say, "I will cry unto thee in all mine afflictions"? (Alma 33:11.)

_____ c. What happened to Zenock? Why?

_____ d. What did the Lord tell Moses to do to protect the people from the fiery serpents? (See Numbers 21:5–9.)

_____ e. Why did the people refuse to look and live?

_____ f. What did Alma desire that his brethren should do?

Alma 34

_____ a. What was the great question in the minds of the Zoramites?

_____ b. What would happen if no atonement were made?

_____ c. What did the law of Moses, which had animal sacrifices, point to?

_____ d. What will mercy do for us when we exercise faith unto repentance?

_____ e. What happens to those who exercise "no faith unto repentance"? (Alma 34:16.)

_____ f. In verses 18 through 26, what did Amulek tell the people to do?

_____ g. What should we do with our hearts when we are not crying unto the Lord?

_____ h. What else must we do if we want our prayers heard and answered?

_____ i. What is this life the time for us to do?

_____ j. What will happen to us "if we do not improve our time while in this life"? (V. 33.)

_____ k. Why is it useless to say "I will repent" just before we die? (V. 34.)

_____ l. Why did Amulek exhort us to "be watchful unto prayer continually"? (V. 39.)

Alma 35

_____ a. Why were the more popular part of the Zoramites angry?

_____ b. Why did the Zoramite leaders gather all the people together?

_____ c. How did the people of Ammon treat those who had been cast out?

_____ d. Where can we read an account of this war? (See Alma 43:3.)

_____ e. Why was Alma's heart "exceedingly sorrowful"? (Alma 35:15.)

_____ f. Why did Alma ask his sons to come to him?

Alma 36

_____ a. To whom was Alma speaking?

_____ b. What will God do for us when we put our trust in him?

_____ c. What happened to Alma for three days and three nights at the time of his conversion? (See also Mosiah 27:24–32.)

_____ d. What did Alma do that caused him "to remember [his] pains no more"? (Alma 36:19.)

_____ e. In what had the Lord given Alma "exceedingly great joy"? (V. 25.)

_____ f. Why must we keep the commandments of God?

Alma 37

_____ a. To whom did Alma give the sacred records?

_____ b. Why had God preserved these records?

_____ c. What would happen to Helaman if he did not obey the commandments of God? if he did obey the commandments of God?

_____ d. Why was Helaman commanded not to reveal the details of the secret combinations of those who were destroyed?

_____ e. What two things did Alma ask his son Helaman to learn in his youth?

_____ f. How did the Liahona work?

_____ g. What did Alma compare the Liahona to?

Alma 38

_____ a. To whom was Alma speaking?

_____ b. What did Shiblon commence to do in his youth?

_____ c. What will happen to us if we put our trust in God?

_____ d. What is the only "way or means whereby [we] can be saved"? (Alma 38:9.)

_____ e. List seven things that Alma counseled his son Shiblon to do.

Alma 39

VERSE NUMBER

_____ a. To whom was Alma speaking?

_____ b. What two things did Alma "have against" his son? (Alma 39:2.)

_____ c. Which sin is most abominable of all sins except shedding innocent blood and denying the Holy Ghost? (See also v. 5a.)

_____ d. What is the unpardonable sin?

_____ e. Why did Alma want his son to repent?

_____ f. What did Alma command his son Corianton to do because of his youth?

_____ g. Why did Alma command his son to do good?

_____ h. Why should we not seek "after riches [or] the vain things of this world"? (V. 14.)

Alma 40

VERSE NUMBER

_____ a. What had Alma "inquired diligently" of the Lord to know? (Alma 40:3.)

_____ b. What happens to the spirits of both the righteous and the wicked between death and the resurrection?

_____ c. What will happen to the soul and the body in the resurrection? (See also Bible Dictionary, p. 761, s.v. "Resurrection.")

_____ d. What happens to the wicked when they die? (See Alma 40:26a.)

Alma 41

VERSE NUMBER

_____ a. What will we be restored to if in this life we have performed good works and had good desires in our hearts? if we have performed evil works?

_____ b. What can wickedness never bring?

_____ c. What is the meaning of the word *restoration?*

_____ d. What is required of us to be restored to mercy, justice, and righteousness?

_____ e. What happens to the good things we do to others?

_____ f. What happens to the bad things we do to others?

Alma 42

VERSE NUMBER

_____ a. What was Corianton also worried about?

_____ b. Why was Adam prevented from returning to the Garden to partake of the fruit?

_____ c. What is spiritual death?

_____ d. What would happen to us when we die if it were not for the plan of redemption?

_____ e. How is the plan of mercy put into effect?

_____ f. What is required for repentance to be available to us?

_____ g. Why are only the truly penitent saved?

_____ h. What will happen to those who have done evil in their lives?

_____ i. What did Alma desire Corianton to do?

_____ j. What was Corianton called of God to do?

_____ k. What charge did Alma give to his son?

Alma 43

_____ a. What did Alma and his sons do among the people?

_____ b. Where did the Nephites gather to fight the Lamanites?

_____ c. Why did Zerahemnah appoint the Amalekites and the Zoramites to be chief captains over the Lamanites?

_____ d. What was the design of the Nephites?

_____ e. How did the people of Ammon support the Nephite army?

_____ f. Who was the chief captain of all the armies of the Nephites?

_____ g. Why did the Lamanites dare not fight the Nephites in the land of Jershon?

_____ h. How did Moroni know where to lead his army?

_____ i. Why did Moroni think it no sin to defend his people by stratagem?

_____ j. How did the Lamanites fight when surrounded by the Nephites?

_____ k. What has the Lord said about defending ourselves and our families?

_____ l. Why did Moroni command his men to stop fighting?

Alma 44

_____ a. What did Moroni say to Zerahemnah?

_____ b. What did Zerahemnah say to Moroni?

_____ c. What was Moroni's reply?

_____ d. What did Zerahemnah do?

_____ e. What did Moroni allow those Lamanites who "entered into a covenant of peace" to do? (Alma 44:15.)

_____ f. Why did Zerahemnah cry "mightily unto Moroni"? (V. 19.)

Alma 45

_____ a. What did the people of Nephi do because of their victory?

_____ b. What did Alma request Helaman to record but not show to the people?

_____ c. Why would the Nephites be destroyed?

_____ d. What did Alma do after he "had said these things to Helaman"? (Alma 45:15.)

_____ e. What was the cause of the dissension in the land?

Alma 46

_____ a. How did Amalickiah persuade many to join him?

_____ b. What did Helaman want us to understand in Alma 46:8 through 10?

_____ c. What did Moroni do when he heard of the dissension?

_____ d. What did he do with the title of liberty?

_____ e. What covenant did the people make with God?

_____ f. Why did Amalickiah take his people out of the land of Nephi?

_____ g. What happened to those captives who "would not enter into a covenant to support the cause of freedom"? (V. 35.)

_____ h. What had God "prepared to remove the cause of diseases"? (V. 40.)

Alma 47

_____ a. Why did the Lamanites fear the proclamation of their king?

_____ b. How did those who rebelled gain control over the king's army?

_____ c. How and why did Lehonti die?

_____ d. How did Amalickiah become leader of the Lamanites?

_____ e. What kind of people were those who changed from Nephites to Lamanites?

Alma 48

_____ a. What goal had Amalickiah reached?

_____ b. What was Amalickiah determined to do?

_____ c. How had Moroni prepared his people?

_____ d. What kind of man was Moroni?

_____ e. What were the Nephites taught about fighting?

_____ f. What did the Nephites believe God would do if they kept the commandments?

_____ g. Why were the Nephites sorry to take up arms against the Lamanites?

Alma 49

_____ a. Why were the chief captains of the Lamanites astonished?

_____ b. Why would the Lamanites have attacked the city if Amalickiah had been with them?

_____ c. How effective was the wisdom of Moroni?

_____ d. What happened to the Lamanites when "they began to dig down [the Nephites'] banks of earth"? (Alma 49:22.) 49:

_____ e. What did Amalickiah swear "with an oath" to do? (V. 27.)

_____ f. Why was there peace and prosperity in the Church?

Alma 50

_____ a. What did Moroni have his armies do during the period of peace?

_____ b. Why did the armies of Moroni increase daily?

_____ c. What caused the Nephite wars and destructions?

_____ d. What started the contention between the people in the land of Morianton and the land of Lehi?

_____ e. Who led the Nephite army after the people of Morianton?

_____ f. Why was Morianton killed and his army taken prisoner?

_____ g. What happened to the people who followed Morianton?

Alma 51

_____ a. Who were the kingmen?

_____ b. Who were the freemen?

_____ c. Who were the people who favored having kings?

_____ d. Why were the kingmen "glad in their hearts" when the Lamanites came to do battle? (Alma 51:13.)

_____ e. What did Moroni do when the kingmen refused to defend their country?

_____ f. Why did the army of Teancum gain the advantage over the Lamanites?

_____ g. How was Teancum able to stop the Lamanite army?

Alma 52

VERSE NUMBER

_____ a. What did the Lamanite army do when they discovered their leader had been killed?

_____ b. Why did Moroni not go to help Teancum?

_____ c. How did Moroni get the Lamanites to leave the city of Mulek?

_____ d. When Moroni and his army entered the city, who did they kill?

_____ e. What did Moroni command his armies to do when they had surrounded the Lamanites?

_____ f. What did Moroni say to the Lamanite army when he saw their confusion?

Alma 53

VERSE NUMBER

_____ a. What did Moroni cause the Lamanite prisoners to do in the city of Bountiful? Why?

_____ b. Why were the Nephites "placed in the most dangerous circumstances"? (Alma 53:9.)

_____ c. Why did the people of Ammon (formerly the anti-Nephi-Lehis) refuse to fight?

_____ d. What covenant had their sons made?

_____ e. How many young men entered into this covenant?

_____ f. Who did these young men choose to be their leader?

_____ g. What kind of young men were the sons of the people of Ammon?

Alma 54

_____ a. Why did Moroni want to exchange prisoners?

_____ b. What did Moroni say in his epistle that made Ammoron angry? ?

_____ c. What reason did Ammoron give for fighting the war?

_____ d. Who was Ammoron descended from?

Alma 55

_____ a. Why was Moroni more angry when he received the epistle from Ammoron?

_____ b. Who was Laman and what did he do?

_____ c. How did Moroni obtain the Nephite captives from the Lamanites?

_____ d. Why did Moroni refrain from slaying the Lamanite guards?

_____ e. How did the Nephites keep from being poisoned?

Alma 56

_____ a. How many years before the coming of Christ did Moroni receive Helaman's epistle?

_____ b. Why were the people of Ammon about to break their covenant not to fight?

_____ c. Why did Helaman prevent them from breaking the covenant?

_____ d. Why did Antipus rejoice when Helaman joined with him?

_____ e. Who brought "many provisions" to the army of Helaman and Antipus? (Alma 56:27.)

_____ f. Why did the Lamanites begin to be fearful concerning the army of Antipus?

_____ g. What did the sons of Helaman say when asked to fight the Lamanites?

_____ h. What had their mothers taught them?

_____ i. How did the sons of Helaman save the Nephite army?

_____ j. How many of the sons of Helaman were slain in the battle? Why?

Alma 57

_____ a. How did Helaman and his army take the city of Cumeni?

_____ b. What did the army of Helaman resolve to do with the Lamanite prisoners?

_____ c. What did the sons of Helaman do when the rest of the "army were about to give way before the Lamanites"? (Alma 57:20.)

_____ d. How many of the sons of Helaman "received many wounds"? (V. 25.)

_____ e. Why were none of the sons of Helaman killed?

_____ f. Why was Helaman filled with "exceeding joy" at hearing the "words of Gid"? (V. 36.)

Alma 58

_____ a. What was the "next object" of Helaman and his army?

_____ b. What indicated there were problems in the Nephite government?

_____ c. What did the army do when the support did not come?

_____ d. What did the Lord do for Helaman's army?

_____ e. Why did the Lamanite army prepare to come out of the city of Manti?

_____ f. What did the Lamanite army do when they returned to the city of Manti?

_____ g. How did Helaman describe his sons in verse 40?

Alma 59

_____ a. List three things that Moroni did immediately after reading Helaman's epistle.

_____ b. What fear did Moroni have when he received the news that Nephihah had been lost?

_____ c. Why did the chief captains also doubt and marvel?

_____ d. Why was Moroni angry with the government?

Alma 60

_____ a. Although the Nephite armies had suffered much because of the lack of food and men, what was an even greater concern to Moroni?

_____ b. What did Moroni believe one of the duties of government to be?

_____ c. Why does the Lord suffer the righteous to be slain? (See also Alma 60:13b.)

_____ d. What group caused the people to suffer all manner of afflictions? Why?

_____ e. What did Moroni threaten do if Pahoran did not send food and men to strengthen the army?

_____ f. What had the Lord said to Moroni about wicked governors?

_____ g. What did Moroni seek?

Alma 61

_____ a. How many people had risen up against Pahoran and the freemen?

_____ b. How did the kingmen lead "away the hearts of many people"? (Alma 61:4.)

_____ c. Why did the Nephite armies fail to receive their provisions and reinforcements?

_____ d. Why did the kingmen refrain from attacking the freemen?

_____ e. What did Pahoran seek?

_____ f. Under what condition would Pahoran put his people in bondage to the Lamanites?

_____ g. Why did Pahoran ask Moroni to go to him?

Alma 62

VERSE NUMBER

_____ a. Who were put to death when Pahoran was restored to the judgment seat?

_____ b. Why was the law of freedom observed so strictly?

_____ c. What did Moroni do to the four thousand Lamanite prisoners?

_____ d. How did Moroni capture the city of Nephihah?

_____ e. Where did the Lamanite army gather together?

_____ f. What happened to Teancum?

_____ g. Why were the Nephites spared?

_____ h. What did Helaman do after the war?

_____ i. What did the Nephites do as a result of the actions of Helaman and his brethren?

Alma 63

VERSE NUMBER

_____ a. Who took possession of the sacred things that Alma had delivered to Helaman?

_____ b. What did Hagoth do?

_____ c. Who did Shiblon give the record to?

_____ d. Who wrote the book of Alma?

HELAMAN

Helaman 1

VERSE NUMBER

_____ a. Why was Paanchi condemned to death?

_____ b. Why did Kishkumen murder Pahoran?

_____ c. What did Kishkumen and his friends do immediately after the murder?

_____ d. Why was Kishkumen not known among the Nephites?

_____ e. Who was Coriantumr?

_____ f. Why did the Lamanites surrender to the Nephites?

Helaman 2

VERSE NUMBER

_____ a. How was Helaman "appointed to fill the judgment seat"? (Helaman 2:2.)

_____ b. How did Gadianton become the leader of the band of Kishkumen?

_____ c. Why did Kishkumen seek to destroy Helaman?

_____ d. How did the servant gain the confidence of Kishkumen?

_____ e. What did the servant discover about the purpose of the Gadianton band?

_____ f. Why was Helaman not able to capture Gadianton?

Helaman 3

_____ a. Why did a great many of the Nephites go to the land northward?

_____ b. What did the Nephites use to build their houses where timber was scarce?

_____ c. What did these people do with the young trees to have timber in the future?

_____ d. Why were the Gadianton robbers established in the land and not destroyed?

_____ e. What entered "into the hearts of the people who professed to belong to the church of God" in "the fifty and first year of the reign of the judges"? (Helaman 3:33.)

_____ f. What did the humble followers of Christ do?

Helaman 4

_____ a. Why did the Lamanites make war on the Nephites?

_____ b. Why was there a "great slaughter" among the Nephites? (Helaman 4:11.)

_____ c. What did the Nephites do out of fear of being destroyed by the Lamanites?

_____ d. Why had the Spirit of the Lord withdrawn from them?

Helaman 5

_____ a. In what way were the Nephites "ripening for destruction"? (Helaman 5:2.)

_____ b. Why did Nephi give up the judgment seat? (See also Alma 31:5.)

_____ c. Why did Helaman name his sons Nephi and Lehi?

_____ d. Why must we build our foundation upon the rock of Christ?

_____ e. How did Nephi and Lehi know what to say when they spoke to the people? (See also Helaman 5:18a.)

_____ f. Describe the voice that spoke to the Lamanites in the prison.

_____ g. What did the voice say the second time?

_____ h. What happened to the Lamanites after they cried unto God with faith?

_____ i. How was the statement in Alma 31:5 proven true in the lives of the converted Lamanites?

Helaman 6

_____ a. In what year did the righteousness of the Lamanites "exceed that of the Nephites"? (Helaman 6:1.)

_____ b. What allowed the Lamanites and Nephites to become "exceedingly rich"? (V. 9.)

_____ c. Why did some "set their hearts upon their riches"? (V. 17.)

_____ d. What did these people do to get more gain?

_____ e. What did the Lamanites do to the Gadianton robbers?

_____ f. What did the Nephites do to the Gadianton robbers?

_____ g. How did Gadianton obtain the secret oaths for his group of robbers?

_____ h. Why did the Spirit of the Lord begin "to withdraw from the Nephites"? (V. 35.)

Helaman 7

_____ a. What did the Gadianton robbers do who filled the judgment seat?

_____ b. How do the prophets feel when the people are wicked?

_____ c. Why had God forsaken the Nephites?

_____ d. Why had the people forgotten their God?

_____ e. What would happen to the Nephites if they did not repent?

_____ f. Why would it be better for the Lamanites than for the Nephites if the Nephites did not repent?

Helaman 8

_____ a. Why were the judges angry with Nephi?

_____ b. List the nine prophets Nephi named who testified of the coming of Christ?

_____ c. Who did Nephi say had murdered the chief judge?

_____ d. What is Satan's purpose? (See also D&C 10:22, 27.)

Helaman 9

_____ a. What did the five men do when they found the chief judge murdered? Why?

_____ b. Why was Nephi "bound and brought before the multitude"? (Helaman 9:19.)

_____ c. What was the second sign that Nephi gave to the people?

_____ d. Why did some of the people say Nephi was a god?

Helaman 10

VERSE NUMBER

_____ a. Why did the Lord bless Nephi?

_____ b. Why was Nephi blessed that whatever he said would come to pass?

_____ c. What message was Nephi commanded to declare to the people?

_____ d. How do we repent? (See D&C 58:43; 64:7.)

_____ e. How did the people receive Nephi and his message?

_____ f. Why could the people not cast Nephi into prison?

Helaman 11

VERSE NUMBER

_____ a. Which group was responsible for all the wars in the land of Nephi?

_____ b. What did Nephi ask the Lord to do to help the people repent?

_____ c. In what part of the land was the famine the most severe?

_____ d. What happened to the band of Gadianton?

_____ e. How did the people receive Nephi and his message after the famine?

_____ f. How did Nephi, Lehi, and their brethren know the true doctrine?

_____ g. Why were the army unable to destroy the Gadianton robbers?

_____ h. Why did the Lord allow the great evil of the Gadianton robbers to come upon the Nephites?

Helaman 12

VERSE NUMBER

_____ a. Why do people harden their hearts and forget the Lord when he blesses them?

_____ b. Why does the Lord chasten and afflict his people?

_____ c. How does Nephi describe the children of men who will not keep the commandments?

_____ d. Why is it a waste of time to look for treasures in the earth that the Lord has cursed? (See also Helaman 13:17–19.)

_____ e. What will happen to those who are not saved at the last day?

Helaman 13

VERSE NUMBER

_____ a. What did the Lord instruct Samuel to do?

_____ b. What was the only way that the people would be saved from destruction?

_____ c. What would the Lord do "because of the hardness of the hearts of the people of the Nephites"? (Helaman 13:8.)

_____ d. Why had the city not been destroyed by fire from heaven?

_____ e. What will happen to the wicked who hide their treasures unto themselves?

_____ f. Why are their riches cursed by the Lord?

_____ g. Who did the people receive as prophets?

_____ h. Why had the people procrastinated the day of their repentance?

Helaman 14

VERSE NUMBER

_____ a. How many years would pass before Christ would be born?

_____ b. What sign did Samuel give of Christ's birth?

_____ c. Why did Samuel preach to the Nephites?

_____ d. Why would Christ have to die?

_____ e. What would happen at the time of Christ's death?

_____ f. Why would these signs be given?

_____ g. How do we show God that we want to return to him?

Helaman 15

_____ a. Why had the Lord prolonged the days of the Lamanites?

_____ b. Why were many Lamanites converted daily?

_____ c. What did the Lord say concerning the Nephites?

Helaman 16

_____ a. What did the people do who believed Samuel? who did not believe Samuel?

_____ b. How did the scriptures begin to be fulfilled in the year 2 B.C.?

_____ c. What did Satan do just before Christ's birth?

3 NEPHI

3 Nephi 1

_____ a. To whom did Nephi, son of Helaman, give the records?

_____ b. Why did the unbelievers set a day apart?

_____ c. What did the Lord tell Nephi?

_____ d. What did the people do who had not believed the prophets when "at the going down of the sun there was no darkness"? (3 Nephi 1:15.)

_____ e. What did Satan do when the star appeared?

_____ f. Why did the Nephites not destroy the Gadianton robbers?

---

3 Nephi 2

_____ a. What effect did Satan have on the people?

_____ b. How did the Nephites begin "to reckon their time"? (3 Nephi 2:8.)

_____ c. Why were the Lamanites and Nephites compelled to join together to fight the Gadianton robbers?

_____ d. How were the Gadianton robbers able to "gain many advantages" over the Nephites? (V. 18.)

---

3 Nephi 3

_____ a. Why was Lachoneus astonished after reading the epistle of Giddianhi?

_____ b. What did Lachoneus have his people do?

_____ c. What did his proclamation tell the Nephites to do?

_____ d. Who was the commander of the Nephite armies?

_____ e. What caused the Nephites to repent and pray to the Lord?

---

3 Nephi 4

_____ a. What problems did the Gadianton robbers face?

_____ b. How many years' worth of supplies had the Nephites gathered?

_____ c. What was the only way the robbers could subsist?

_____ d. Who did the Nephites fear more than they feared the robbers?

_____ e. Why did the siege not work?

_____ f. Why were the Nephites delivered from destruction?

3 Nephi 5

_____ a. What did the Nephites do as a result of their knowledge of God?

_____ b. What did the Nephites do with the prisoners who had been captured? (See also 3 Nephi 5:4a.)

_____ c. Who prepared the Nephite record for Joseph Smith to translate? (See also v. 12a.)

3 Nephi 6

_____ a. How had the laws of the Nephites been formed?

_____ b. What was the only thing that could "hinder the people from prospering continually"?

_____ c. How did the people begin to be distinguished?

_____ d. What effect did this have upon the Church?

_____ e. What was the cause of the Nephites' iniquity?

_____ f. Why were the Nephites in a state of awful wickedness?

_____ g. Who became angry at the prophets?

_____ h. Who gave and administered the covenant the lawyers and judges made?

_____ i. What three things did they covenant to do?

---

3 Nephi 7

_____ a. What did the people do when the chief judge was murdered?

_____ b. Why were the laws, or regulations, of the government destroyed?

_____ c. Who was the leader of the secret combination?

_____ d. Why did Jacob and his people flee to the north?

_____ e. List four things we learn about Nephi in 3 Nephi 7:15?

_____ f. Why were the people angry with Nephi?

_____ g. Who ministered to Nephi daily because of his great faith in Jesus?

_____ h. What did Nephi do for his brother? (See also v. 19*b*.)

_____ i. Why were all who repented "baptized with water"? (V. 25.)

---

3 Nephi 8

_____ a. Who were the only ones who could do miracles in the name of Jesus?

_____ b. How long did the storm and earthquakes last?

_____ c. How great was the darkness that covered the land?

_____ d. How long did the darkness last?

_____ e. Why did the people mourn?

---

3 Nephi 9

_____ a. What happened to "the people of king Jacob," who had destroyed the Nephite government? (See also 3 Nephi 7:12.)

_____ b. Why were some of the people spared from destruction?

_____ c. What kind of sacrifice did the Lord require after the law of Moses was fulfilled?

_____ d. Who will the Lord receive?

---

3 Nephi 10

_____ a. Why did the people cease howling and lamenting?

_____ b. Why could the Lord not gather the people "as a hen gathereth her chickens"?

_____ c. What did the earth do after three days and after the darkness dispersed?

_____ d. Which part of the people was saved?

_____ e. What would Nephi show unto us?

---

3 Nephi 11

_____ a. Where did the multitude gather?

_____ b. Describe the voice that spoke to the people.

_____ c. Whose voice did the people hear? (See also 3 Nephi 11:7a.)

_____ d. Who was the man descending out of heaven clothed in a white robe?

_____ e. Why did the people feel the Savior's wounds?

_____ f. What power did the Lord give to Nephi?

_____ g. How were the people to be baptized?

_____ h. Why did the Lord require that there be no disputations among the people?

_____ i. What is the doctrine of Jesus and his Father?

---

3 Nephi 12

_____ a. How many disciples did Christ choose to minister to the people?

_____ b. Who will the pure in heart see?

_____ c. How do we let our light shine before men?

_____ d. When we have a disagreement with our brother, what should we do before going to the Lord?

_____ e. How should we treat our enemies who hate or persecute us?

_____ f. What is the difference between 3 Nephi 12:48 and Matthew 5:48?

---

3 Nephi 13

_____ a. How should we help the poor?

_____ b. How should we pray?

_____ c. What will happen if we do not forgive others?

_____ d. How should we fast?

_____ e. What kind of riches should we seek? Why?

_____ f. What counsel did Jesus give specifically to the twelve disciples he had chosen?

---

3 Nephi 14

_____ a. Why should we refrain from judging others harshly?

_____ b. Why should we refrain from criticizing our brother for his faults?

_____ c. How should we deal with our problems in life?

_____ d. Which verse contains the Golden Rule?

_____ e. Why are there few that find eternal life?

_____ f. How can we tell good people from evil people?

_____ g. What is required if we are to enter the kingdom of heaven?

_____ h. Why does a wise man build his house upon a rock? (See also 3 Nephi 14:25a.)

3 Nephi 15

_____ a. Who will Jesus "raise up at the last day"? (3 Nephi 15:1.)

_____ b. To whom will Jesus give eternal life?

_____ c. When Jesus taught the people in Jerusalem, why did he refer to the Nephites as "other sheep"? (See also John 10:14–16.)

3 Nephi 16

_____ a. Where did Jesus say he would go next? (See 3 Nephi 16:3b.)

_____ b. Why did Jesus command the Nephites to record his sayings?

_____ c. Why would the Church be restored through the Gentiles?

_____ d. What would happen to those Gentiles who "will not turn unto [the Lord], and hearken unto [his] voice?" (V. 15; see 3 Nephi 20:16.)

3 Nephi 17

_____ a. What did Jesus ask the people to do after he left?

_____ b. Why did Jesus heal the sick and afflicted?

_____ c. What other group did Jesus command be brought before him?

_____ d. What testimony did the people bear who "saw and heard" Jesus pray to the Father? (3 Nephi 17:16.)

_____ e. What did the little children experience that day?

_____ f. How many men, women, and children witnessed these things?

3 Nephi 18

VERSE NUMBER

_____ a. To whom should the bread and wine of the sacrament be given?

_____ b. Why did Jesus command that the bread be blessed and eaten?

_____ c. Why did Jesus command that the wine be blessed and drunk?

_____ d. What happens to those who do not build upon the rock?

_____ e. Why is it important to "watch and pray always"? (3 Nephi 18:15.)

_____ f. What promise did Jesus make when we pray for things that are right?

_____ g. Why is family prayer important?

_____ h. What commandment did Jesus give to the disciples? Why?

_____ i. What are we to do with the unworthy among us who will not repent? Why?

3 Nephi 19

VERSE NUMBER

_____ a. Why did many of the people "labor exceedingly all that night"? (3 Nephi 19:3.)

_____ b. What did the twelve disciples teach the twelve groups?

_____ c. When the people prayed, what did they desire most?

_____ d. What happened when the twelve disciples were baptized?

_____ e. Why did Jesus choose these men to be his disciples?

_____ f. Why did Heavenly Father give the disciples the Holy Ghost?

_____ g. How did Heavenly Father know of the disciples' belief?

_____ h. How did the disciples know what to pray for?

_____ i. Why were the Nephites shown such great miracles?

---

3 Nephi 20

_____ a. How was the bread and wine provided?

_____ b. What will happen in the latter days when the remnants of the house of Israel are gathered?

_____ c. Who will afflict those Gentiles who will not repent?

_____ d. Who will be in the New Jerusalem?

_____ e. What covenant did the Lord make with his people?

---

3 Nephi 21

_____ a. What was to be the sign that the Father had commenced to fulfill his covenants that he made with the house of Israel?

_____ b. Why did the Father establish America to be a free land?

_____ c. Why was the Book of Mormon given to the Gentiles first?

_____ d. What is the name of the city that is to be built in the last days? (See also D&C 84:2–4.)

_____ e. Which verses in 3 Nephi 21 describe the preaching of the gospel and the gathering of the house of Israel in the last days?

---

3 Nephi 22

_____ a. What will be established in the last days?

_____ b. How will Israel be gathered?

_____ c. What did the Lord swear "should no more go over the earth"? (3 Nephi 22:9.)

_____ d. Who will teach the children when Israel is gathered?

---

3 Nephi 23

_____ a. Why did Jesus command the people to search the words of Isaiah diligently?

_____ b. Of what had Jesus commanded Samuel the Lamanite to testify to the people?

_____ c. What did Jesus command should be recorded?

---

3 Nephi 24

_____ a. What did Jesus command the Nephites to write? (See also Bible Dictionary, p. 728, s.v. "Malachi.")

_____ b. How do we rob God?

_____ c. What will the Lord do for us when we pay our tithing?

_____ d. Whose names are recorded in the Lord's book of remembrance?

---

3 Nephi 25

_____ a. What will happen to the proud and wicked at the Second Coming?

_____ b. When would Elijah come? (See D&C 110:13–16.)

_____ c. Which verse in 3 Nephi 25 describes the mission of Elijah as family history and temple work?

---

3 Nephi 26

_____ a. Why did Jesus give the words of Malachi to the Nephites?

_____ b. What did Jesus teach to the people?

_____ c. Why did Mormon not record all the teachings of Jesus?

_____ d. What did the children say when their tongues had been loosed?

_____ e. List five things that happened to those who were baptized.

---

3 Nephi 27

_____ a. What were the people doing when Jesus appeared to them?

_____ b. By what name did Jesus command the people to call his church? (See also 3 Nephi 26:21.)

_____ c. What is the gospel of Jesus Christ?

_____ d. How do we enter the kingdom of God?

_____ e. Why did the Father, Jesus, and all the holy angels rejoice?

_____ f. Why was Jesus sad?

---

3 Nephi 28

_____ a. What did nine of the disciples desire?

_____ b. What did three of the disciples desire?

_____ c. With what did Jesus bless these three?

_____ d. What did the Three Nephites experience during their missionary labors?

_____ e. How did Mormon know of the existence of the Three Nephites?

_____ f. What change was made upon the Three Nephites?

3 Nephi 29

_____ a. What will happen when "these sayings [the Book of Mormon] shall come unto the Gentiles"? (3 Nephi 29:1.)

_____ b. Why should we not spurn or make fun of the Jews?

3 Nephi 30

_____ a. Who commanded that verse 1 of 3 Nephi 30 be written?

_____ b. What are the Gentiles in the latter days to do? Why?

4 NEPHI

4 Nephi 1

_____ a. How many people were not converted by A.D. 36?

_____ b. Describe how the people lived in that year.

_____ c. What miracles were performed by the disciples?

_____ d. Why was there "no contention in the land" after one hundred years had passed away?

_____ e. How did the people feel?

_____ f. To whom did Nephi give the records?

_____ g. What did some of the people begin doing in the year 201 A.D.?

_____ h. What effect did this have upon the people?

_____ i. Why did the false churches grow so quickly?

_____ j. What effect did the miracles performed by the Three Nephites have on the people?

_____ k. What happened among the people in the year A.D. 231?

_____ l. What caused the disciples "to sorrow for the sins of the world"? (4 Nephi 1:44.)

MORMON

Mormon 1

VERSE NUMBER

_____ a. Who was Ammaron? (See also 4 Nephi 1:47–48.)

_____ b. What was Mormon instructed to do when he was about twenty-four years old?

_____ c. Why did the Lord remove the Three Nephites from the people? (See also Mormon 8:10.)

_____ d. Why was Mormon forbidden to preach unto the people?

_____ e. Whose power "was wrought upon all the face of the land"? (Mormon 1:19.)

Mormon 2

_____ a. How old was Mormon when he became leader of the Nephite armies?

_____ b. Why did the Nephite armies "retreat towards the north countries"? (Mormon 2:3.)

_____ c. Why was no one able to "keep that which was his own"? (See also v. 10a.)

_____ d. Why was the joy of Mormon in vain?

_____ e. Why did the Nephites at the city of Shem stand boldly before the Lamanites and not flee?

_____ f. How large was Mormon's army that defeated the Lamanites?

Mormon 3

_____ a. How did Mormon know the Lamanites were preparing for war?

_____ b. What great evil did the Nephites do after their victory that caused Mormon to refuse to be their leader?

_____ c. What did the Lord say about their wickedness?

_____ d. Who will judge the twelve disciples whom Jesus called in this land?

_____ e. Who must "stand before the judgment seat of Christ"? (Mormon 3:20.)

Mormon 4

_____ a. Why did the Lamanites begin to have power over the Nephites?

_____ b. Who punished the wicked?

_____ c. How hard were the hearts of both Nephites and Lamanites?

_____ d. What did the Lamanites do with the women and children they had taken prisoner after battles at Teancum and Boaz?

Mormon 5

VERSE NUMBER

_____ a. How much hope did Mormon have that he could deliver the Nephites from destruction? Why?

_____ b. What happened to "those whose flight was swifter than the Lamanites' "?

_____ c. Why will the Book of Mormon go to "the unbelieving of the Jews"? (Mormon 5:7.)

_____ d. Who were the people "led about by"? (V. 18.)

Mormon 6

VERSE NUMBER

_____ a. What did Mormon desire of the king of the Lamanites?

_____ b. Where did Mormon gather all his people?

_____ c. Where did Mormon hide the sacred records?

_____ d. Why was every Nephite soul "filled with terror" when the Lamanite army approached? (Mormon 6:8.)

_____ e. How many of the 230,000-man Nephite army were alive "on the morrow"? (V. 11.)

Mormon 7

VERSE NUMBER

_____ a. Who was Mormon writing to? (See Mormon 7:1.)

_____ b. What must the Lamanites do in the latter days to be saved?

_____ c. What is the fate of those "found guiltless before him at the judgment day"? (V. 7.)

Mormon 8

_____ a. Who was now keeping the record?

_____ b. What was the fate of the Nephites who had escaped to the south?

_____ c. What happened to Mormon?

_____ d. How many years had passed since the coming of the Savior?

_____ e. Who were the Lamanites now fighting?

_____ f. How did Moroni know of the Three Nephites?

_____ g. Who would have power to bring the Book of Mormon to light in the last days? (See also Mormon 8:14b.)

_____ h. What will be the fate of those who fight against the work of God?

_____ i. What would the world be like when the Book of Mormon was published?

_____ j. How was Moroni able to speak to us as if he were with us? (See also Mormon 9:30.)

_____ k. How did Moroni describe the people of our day?

Mormon 9

_____ a. To whom was Moroni speaking?

_____ b. Where will those who have a consciousness of their guilt feel more comfortable? Why?

_____ c. Why does God cease to do miracles among the children of men?

_____ d. What is the promise that "is unto all, even unto the ends of the earth"? (Mormon 9:21.)

_____ e. What should we be doing in the days of our probation? (See vv. 27–29.)

_____ f. What should we do instead of condemning others' imperfections?

ETHER

Ether 1

_____ a. What is the name of the tower mentioned in Ether 1:3 and 33? (See also Genesis 11:1–9.)

_____ b. Who included the book of Ether in the record of the Nephites?

_____ c. What is contained in the first part of the plates that Moroni did not record?

_____ d. Who wrote the record on the twenty-four plates?

_____ e. What three things did Jared ask his brother to ask of the Lord?

_____ f. What did the Lord command the group to do?

_____ g. Why did the Lord bless them?

Ether 2

_____ a. List five things the people took with them.

_____ b. How did they know where to travel?

_____ c. Who will possess the land of promise?

_____ d. When will the fulness of God's wrath come upon the people in America?

_____ e. Why did Mormon say this record would come to us?

_____ f. What does God require of the people if they are to be free?

_____ g. Why did the Lord chasten the brother of Jared for three hours?

_____ h. How did the people know how to build the barges?

_____ i. How did the brother of Jared provide fresh air in the barges?

Ether 3

_____ a. How many vessels were made?

_____ b. What had the Lord done to the group because of their iniquity?

_____ c. What did the brother of Jared ask the Lord to do so that they would have light in their boats?

_____ d. Why did the brother of Jared fall down, having been "struck with fear"? (Ether 3:6.)

_____ e. How was the brother of Jared able to see "the finger of the Lord"? (V. 6.)

_____ f. Why was the brother of Jared afraid when he had seen the Lord's body of flesh and bones?

_____ g. Why could the brother of Jared "not be kept from beholding within the veil"? (V. 19.)

_____ h. Why did the brother of Jared no longer have faith after seeing the finger of the Lord?

_____ i. Which inhabitants of the earth did the Lord show to the brother of Jared? Why?

Ether 4

VERSE NUMBER

_____ a. Why did King Mosiah not translate this record for his people?

_____ b. When are these things to "go forth unto the Gentiles"? (Ether 4:6.)

_____ c. What will happen if we believe the things which the Lord has spoken?

_____ d. Where does that which "persuadeth [us] to do good" come from? (V. 12.)

_____ e. Why is great knowledge hidden from us?

_____ f. What will have commenced when we receive the Book of Mormon?

Ether 5

VERSE NUMBER

_____ a. To how many would God show the plates so "they shall know of a surety that these things are true"? (Ether 5:3; see also D&C 17:3–5.)

_____ b. What is required of us to be received into the kingdom of God?

_____ c. When will we know that Moroni had authority for "these things"? (Ether 5:6.)

Ether 6

VERSE NUMBER

_____ a. Why were the barges "tossed upon the waves" and "many times buried in the depths of the sea"? (Ether 6:5–6.)

_____ b. For how many days did the Jaredites travel upon the water to the promised land?

_____ c. What was the first thing the Jaredites did after they reached the promised land?

_____ d. What did the people desire of Jared and his brother before they died?

_____ e. Why was the request "grievous unto them"? (V. 23.)

_____ f. What did King Orihah teach the people?

Ether 7

_____ a. Who did Corihor take captive?

_____ b. What two things was Shule, the son of Kib, mighty in?

_____ c. How did Shule execute judgment after he had been made king?

_____ d. Who saved Shule from being put to death by Noah?

_____ e. What were the names of the two kingdoms when the country was divided?

_____ f. How did the people receive the prophets while Shule was king?

_____ g. What did King Shule give the prophets?

_____ h. Why did the Lord spare the people in the kingdom of Shule?

Ether 8

_____ a. How did Jared obtain half of his father's kingdom?

_____ b. What did Jared do with his father after he defeated him in battle?

_____ c. Why did Jared become "exceedingly sorrowful"? (Ether 8:7.)

_____ d. What did the people of old obtain "by their secret plans"? (V. 9.)

_____ e. What did Jared require in order for Akish to take his daughter for a wife?

_____ f. By what power are the secret oaths kept up?

_____ g. What did Jared and Akish form that "is most abominable and wicked above all, in the sight of God"? (V. 18.)

_____ h. What effect did these secret combinations have on the Nephites and on the Jaredites?

_____ i. What will happen to nations that uphold secret combinations?

_____ j. Why is it "wisdom in God that these things should be shown unto [us]"? (V. 23.)

_____ k. Who is the author of the secret combinations?

Ether 9

VERSE NUMBER

_____ a. How was the Lord "merciful unto Omer" the king? (Ether 9:2.)

_____ b. What happened to Jared after he had given his daughter to Akish?

_____ c. How was the kingdom of Akish destroyed?

_____ d. Who did Emer see after he had given up his kingdom to his son Coriantum?

_____ e. How old was Coriantum when he died?

_____ f. How did Heth become king?

_____ g. How did the Lord warn the people to repent?

_____ h. What did King Heth command the people do to the prophets?

_____ i. What did the Lord do to humble the people and help them to repent?

_____ j. What did the people do when they saw they were about to perish?

Ether 10

VERSE NUMBER

_____ a. What happened to the wicked King Heth?

_____ b. What happened to Shez after he rebelled against his father, King Shez?

_____ c. What happened to Riplakish after he had reigned for forty-two years?

_____ d. Why did the people anoint Morianton to be their king?

_____ e. Why was Morianton cut off from the Lord?

_____ f. What happened in the days of Lib?

_____ g. What happened in the days of Com?

Ether 11

_____ a. How did the Lord warn the people in the days of Com that they would be destroyed if they did not repent?

_____ b. How did the people receive the warning?

_____ c. What great wickedness did the brother of Shiblom cause?

_____ d. Why did the people begin to repent of their iniquity in the days of Shiblom?

_____ e. What happened to King Shiblom?

_____ f. Why did the prophets mourn and withdraw from the people in the days of Ether?

_____ g. What did the prophets prophesy in the days of Coriantor?

_____ h. Why did the people "reject all the words of the prophets" in the days of Coriantor? (Ether 11:22.)

Ether 12

_____ a. Who was the prophet that came "in the days of Coriantumr"? (Ether 12:1.)

_____ b. What is faith?

_____ c. Why should we not deny things that we do not understand?

_____ d. When can there be no miracles shown to the people?

_____ e. Who have the performers of miracles first believed in?

_____ f. What was one of the weaknesses of the Nephites?

_____ g. What was one of the strengths of the brother of Jared?

_____ h. What was one of the strengths of the Nephites?

_____ i. What did the Lord say of fools who mock?

_____ j. Why did the Lord give us weaknesses?

_____ k. How can we overcome our weaknesses?

_____ l. What did the brother of Jared do to Mount Zerin through faith?

_____ m. What did the Lord show to his disciples who had faith?

_____ n. What are two things we must have to inherit a "house . . . even among the mansions of [the] Father"? (V. 32.)

_____ o. What did the Lord tell Moroni when he prayed that the Gentiles would have charity?

_____ p. How did Moroni know all these things?

Ether 13

_____ a. Upon what land will the New Jerusalem be built?

_____ b. What will the New Jerusalem be for the Lord?

_____ c. Who will dwell in the New Jerusalem?

_____ d. What did Ether do when he was cast out from the people?

_____ e. How did the mighty men seek to destroy Coriantumr?

_____ f. What did the Lord command Ether to say when he returned to Coriantumr?

_____ g. How did Coriantumr and the people receive his message?

_____ h. Why did Coriantumr not go to battle for two years?

Ether 14

_____ a. Why did every man keep the hilt of his sword in his right hand?

_____ b. Who was the brother of Shared who fought with Coriantumr and placed himself upon the thone of Coriantumr?

_____ c. Who murdered Gilead as he sat on the throne?

_____ d. Who murdered the high priest in a secret pass?

_____ e. What troubled the people by day and by night?

_____ f. Why did Shiz command his armies not to pursue the armies of Coriantumr?

Ether 15

_____ a. How many of Coriantumr's men had been slain in the wars?

_____ b. Why did Shiz and Coriantumr continue the war after writing each other?

_____ c. What is another name for the hill Ramah? (See Mormon 6:6.)

_____ d. How long did the armies prepare for war? Why?

_____ e. Who had full power over the hearts of the people? Why?

_____ f. After eight days of fighting, when all had been killed except Coriantumr and Shiz, what did Coriantumr do? What did Shiz do?

_____ g. What happened to Coriantumr after he "fell to the earth"? (Ether 15:32; see Omni 1:21.)

_____ h. What were the last words of Ether?

MORONI

Moroni 1

_____ a. With whom were the Lamanite wars "exceedingly fierce"? (Moroni 1:2.)

_____ b. What did the Lamanites do because of their hatred?

_____ c. Why was Moroni very careful about where he went?

_____ d. Why did Moroni write "a few more things"? (V. 4.)

Moroni 2

_____ a. What power did Jesus bestow upon his twelve disciples?

_____ b. When was this power bestowed upon them?

Moroni 3

_____ a. What were the disciples called in the Church?

_____ b. In whose name were the priests and teachers ordained?

_____ c. What were they ordained to do?

Moroni 4

_____ a. Why do we partake of the sacramental bread?

_____ b. What will the Father do for those who keep this covenant?

Moroni 5

_____ a. Why do we drink the sacramental water?

_____ b. What will the Father do for those who keep this covenant?

Moroni 6

_____ a. Beginning with verse 2, list four requirements for being baptized.

_____ b. How were the people cleansed after baptism?

_____ c. Why did the Church "meet together oft"? (Moroni 6:5.)

_____ d. What happened to those who committed iniquity but did not confess nor repent?

_____ e. By what power were their meetings conducted?

Moroni 7

_____ a. To whom was Moroni speaking?

_____ b. How profitable are prayers that are offered without real intent?

_____ c. Why is an evil person not able to do good?

_____ d. What does the devil invite and entice you to do?

_____ e. What does that which is of God invite and entice you to do?

_____ f. How are we to know good from evil? (See also Bible Dictionary, p. 649, s.v. "Conscience"; p. 725, s.v. "Light of Christ.")

_____ g. Who are they that "persuadeth no man to do good, no, not one"? (Moroni 7:17.)

_____ h. To whom do angels minister?

_____ i. What does an angel do? (See also Bible Dictionary, p. 608, s.v. "Angels.")

_____ j. What should we hope for?

_____ k. What is charity? (See also Bible Dictionary, p. 632, s.v. "Charity.")

_____ l. For what are you to "pray unto the Father with all the energy of heart"? (Moroni 7:48.)

Moroni 8

VERSE NUMBER

_____ a. Why are little children "not capable of committing sin"? (Moroni 8:11; see D&C 29:47.)

_____ b. What is the age when children become accountable for their actions? (See D&C 68:25–27.)

_____ c. Mormon wrote that "repentance is unto them that are" what? (Moroni 9:9.)

_____ d. What is the "first fruits of repentance"? (V. 25.)

_____ e. What does baptism come by?

_____ f. What does "fulfilling the commandments" bring? (V. 25.)

_____ g. What does the "remission of sins" bring? (V. 26.)

_____ h. What does the Holy Ghost do?

_____ i. What caused the destruction of the Nephites?

Moroni 9

_____ a. Why did Mormon fear that the Lamanites would destroy the Nephites?

_____ b. What did Mormon counsel his son Moroni to do in spite of the condition of the people? Why?

_____ c. What is "most dear and precious above all things"? (Moroni 9:9.)

_____ d. How strong had the Nephites become "in their perversion"? (V. 19.)

_____ e. What was the effect on the women and children?

_____ f. Why could Mormon not recommend the Nephites to God?

_____ g. What would cause the Nephites to perish?

_____ h. What did Mormon want to "rest in [Moroni's] mind forever"? (V. 25.)

Moroni 10

_____ a. To whom was Moroni writing?

_____ b. To know the truth of the Book of Mormon, what must we do? What will Heavenly Father do?

_____ c. How can we "know the truth of all things"? (Moroni 10:5; see also Bible Dictionary, p. 704, s.v. "Holy Ghost.")

_____ d. What are some of the gifts that God gives to his children?

_____ e. From whom does "every good gift" come? (Moroni 10:18.)

_____ f. What is required to "be saved in the kingdom of God"? (V. 21.)

_____ g. Why does despair come?

_____ h. In verses 32 through 33, what does Moroni exhort us to do?

_____ i. Where will we meet Moroni?

Answers

Title Page
a. lines 3 and 4
b. paragraph 2
c. Bible Dictionary, p. 679
d. Bible Dictionary, p. 713

Introduction
a. paragraph 3
b. paragraph 6
c. paragraph 8

The Testimony of Three Witnesses and the Testimony of Eight Witnesses
a. paragraphs 1–2

Testimony of the Prophet Joseph Smith
a. paragraphs 2–3

A Brief Explanation about the Book of Mormon
a. paragraph 1
b. paragraph 4

1 Nephi 1
a. 1
b. 3
c. 2 Chronicles 36:11
d. 5–6
e. 18–19
f. 20

1 Nephi 2
a. 1–3
b. 600 B.C.
c. 4, 11
d. 11–13

e. 16, 19
f. 22

1 Nephi 3
a. 5, 7
b. 15
c. 25
d. 29
e. 31

1 Nephi 4
a. 4
b. 6
c. 10–13
d. 10, 14–17
e. 20–21
f. 28
g. 37

1 Nephi 5
a. 4–6
b. 9–10
c. 11–14
d. 17–19
e. 21

1 Nephi 6
a. 2
b. 4
c. 5–6

1 Nephi 7
a. 1
b. 4–5
c. 8–15, 16, 21
d. 22

1 Nephi 8
a. 3, 4, 17–18, 35–36
b. 23–24
c. 37–38

1 Nephi 9
a. 3, 5

b. 2, 4

1 Nephi 10
a. 4
b. 7–10
c. 12
d. 17
e. 19
f. 20–21
g. 22

1 Nephi 11
a. 6
b. Luke 1:34
c. 20–21
d. 21–22
e. 25
f. 33
g. 36

1 Nephi 12
a. 6
b. 17
c. 17
d. 18
e. 19

1 Nephi 13
a. 6
b. 12, 13–14, 16–19
c. 25–28
d. 29
e. Book of Mormon

1 Nephi 14
a. 1–2
b. 3
c. 7
d. 10–11, 12
e. 14
f. 25–27

1 Nephi 15
a. 2–3
b. 5
c. 8
d. 18
e. 23–24
f. 25
g. 33–35

1 Nephi 16
a. 2
b. 4–5
c. Alma 37:38
d. 18–23
e. 23–32
f. 28–29
g. 37–39

1 Nephi 17
a. 2
b. 3
c. 4
d. 5–6
e. 8–9
f. 17–18
g. 35, 40
h. 45
i. 48–52
j. 53–55

1 Nephi 18
a. 3
b. 9–10
c. 10–11
d. 20
e. 20
f. 25

1 Nephi 19
a. 1
b. 4

Alma 40
a. 3
b. 11–14
c. 23
d. 26

Alma 41
a. 3–8
b. 10
c. 12–13
d. 14
e. 15
f. 15

Alma 42
a. 1
b. 3–4
c. 9
d. 10–12
e. 15, 23
f. 16–18
g. 23–24
h. 28
i. 29–30
j. 31
k. 31

Alma 43
a. 1–2
b. 4
c. 6–8
d. 9
e. 13
f. 16
g. 19–22
h. 23–24
i. 29–30
j. 44
k. 45–47
l. 52–54

Alma 44
a. 1–7
b. 8–9
c. 10–11
d. 12
e. 15
f. 19

Alma 45
a. 1
b. 9–14
c. 12
d. 15–18
e. 23–24

Alma 46
a. 3–5
b. 8–10
c. 11–13
d. 19–20
e. 22
f. 29
g. 35
h. 40

Alma 47
a. 1–3
b. 4–17
c. 18–19
d. 20–31
e. 36

Alma 48
a. 2–3
b. 4
c. 7–10
d. 11–13, 17–18
e. 14
f. 15–16
g. 22–23

Alma 49
a. 5–9
b. 10
c. 15
d. 21–24
e. 27
f. 30

Alma 50
a. 1
b. 12
c. 20–21
d. 26–27
e. 35
f. 35
g. 36

Alma 51
a. 5
b. 6
c. 8
d. 13
e. 14–21
f. 30–32
g. 33–37

Alma 52
a. 1–2
b. 11–12
c. 21–26

d. 25
e. 32
f. 37–38

Alma 53
a. 3–5
b. 9
c. 11–15
d. 17
e. 18
f. 19
g. 20–21

Alma 54
a. 2–3
b. 7
c. 16–17
d. 23

Alma 55
a. 1
b. 4–15
c. 15–24
d. 19
e. 31–32

Alma 56
a. bottom right-hand corner, p. 348
b. 7
c. 8
d. 10, 17
e. 27
f. 29
g. 44–46
h. 47–48
i. 50–52
j. 55–56

Alma 57
a. 7–12
b. 16
c. 19–22
d. 25
e. 26–27
f. 36

Alma 58
a. 1
b. 4–9, 34–36
c. 10–13
d. 11
e. 15
f. 29–30
g. 40

Alma 59
a. 2–4
b. 11
c. 12
d. 13

Alma 60
a. 3–5
b. 8–10
c. 13
d. 16–17
e. 27–30, 35
f. 33
g. 36

Alma 61
a. 3
b. 4
c. 4–5
d. 6–7
e. 9
f. 12–13
g. 15–19

Alma 62
a. 9–11
b. 10
c. 15–17
d. 18–26
e. 33
f. 35–36
g. 40
h. 45–46
i. 48–52

Alma 63
a. 1
b. 5–8
c. 11, 13
d. 17

Helaman 1
a. 5–9
b. 9
c. 10–11
d. 12
e. 15
f. 31–32

Helaman 2
a. 2
b. 4–5
c. 5
d. 7
e. 8
f. 10–11

Helaman 3
a. 3
b. 7
c. 9
d. 23
e. 33
f. 34–35

Helaman 4
a. 1–4
b. 11–14
c. 15, 20
d. 21–25

Helaman 5
a. 2
b. 4
c. 6–7
d. 12
e. 18
f. 29–33
g. 32
h. 42–50
i. 51–52

Helaman 6
a. 1 (29 B.C.) bottom right-hand corner, p. 381
b. 8–9
c. 17
d. 17
e. 20, 37
f. 21–24, 38
g. 26–30
h. 35

Helaman 7
a. 4–5
b. 6–9
c. 17–18
d. 20–21
e. 22, 28
f. 23–24

Helaman 8
a. 4
b. 13–23
c. 27
d. 28

Helaman 9
a. 3–5
b. 19–20
c. 24–36
d. 41

Helaman 10
a. 4–5
b. 5
c. 11
d. Doctrine and Covenants 58:43; 64:7
e. 15, 18
f. 16

Helaman 11
a. 1–2
b. 4–5
c. 6
d. 10
e. 18
f. 23
g. 30–33
h. 34

Helaman 12
a. 2
b. 3
c. 7–8
d. 18–19
e. 25

Helaman 13
a. 3
b. 6, 10–11
c. 8
d. 13–14
e. 18–20
f. 21–23
g. 27–28
h. 38

Helaman 14
a. 2
b. 3–8
c. 9, 11–13
d. 15–18
e. 20–27
f. 28–29
g. 30–31

Helaman 15
a. 4, 10
b. 5–6
c. 17

Helaman 16
a. 1–7
b. 13–14
c. 22–23

3 Nephi 1
a. 2

b. 9
c. 11–14
d. 15–18
e. 21–22
f. 27

3 Nephi 2
a. 2–3
b. 8
c. 11–12
d. 18–19

3 Nephi 3
a. 11
b. 12
c. 13
d. 18–19
e. 25

3 Nephi 4
a. 2–4
b. 4
c. 5
d. 10
e. 18–23
f. 33

3 Nephi 5
a. 3
b. 4–6
c. 10–12

3 Nephi 6
a. 4
b. 5
c. 12
d. 13–14
e. 15–16
f. 18
g. 21
h. 28
i. 29–30

3 Nephi 7
a. 2–3
b. 6
c. 9
d. 12–13
e. 15
f. 18–20
g. 18
h. 19
i. 24–25

3 Nephi 8
a. 1
b. 19

c. 20–22
d. 23
e. 23–25

3 Nephi 9
a. 9
b. 13
c. 20
d. 22

3 Nephi 10
a. 1–2
b. 5
c. 9–10
d. 12
e. 18–19

3 Nephi 11
a. 1
b. 3
c. 6–7
d. 8–10
e. 14–15
f. 18–21
g. 23–26
h. 28–30
i. 31–39

3 Nephi 12
a. 1
b. 8
c. 16
d. 23–24
e. 43–45
f. 48; Matthew 5:48

3 Nephi 13
a. 1–4
b. 5–13
c. 14–15
d. 16–18
e. 19–24
f. 25–34

3 Nephi 14
a. 1–2
b. 3
c. 7–8
d. 12
e. 13–14
f. 15–20
g. 21–23
h. 24–27

3 Nephi 15
a. 1
b. 9

b. 5
c. 6

Ether 6
a. 6
b. 11
c. 12
d. 22
e. 23
f. 30

Ether 7
a. 3–5
b. 7–8
c. 11
d. 18
e. 20
f. 23–24
g. 24–25
h. 26

Ether 8
a. 2
b. 3
c. 7
d. 9
e. 11–12
f. 16
g. 18
h. 20–21
i. 22–24
j. 23
k. 25–26

Ether 9
a. 2–3
b. 5
c. 7–13
d. 22
e. 24
f. 26–27
g. 28
h. 29
i. 30
j. 34–35

Ether 10
a. 1
b. 3
c. 8
d. 9–10
e. 11
f. 19–29
g. 32–34

Ether 11
a. 1
b. 2
c. 5
d. 6–8
e. 9
f. 13
g. 20–21
h. 22

Ether 12
a. 1–2
b. 6
c. 6
d. 12
e. 18
f. 23
g. 24
h. 25
i. 26
j. 27
k. 27
l. 30
m. 31
n. 32–34
o. 36–37
p. 39

Ether 13
a. 2–3, 6
b. 3
c. 10
d. 13–14
e. 15
f. 20–21
g. 22
h. 30–31

Ether 14
a. 1–2
b. 8
c. 9
d. 10
e. 21–23
f. 31

Ether 15
a. 2
b. 6
c. Mormon 6:6
d. 13–14
e. 19
f. 29–31
g. Omni 1:21
h. 34

Moroni 1
a. 2
b. 2
c. 3
d. 4

Moroni 2
a. 2
b. 3

Moroni 3
a. 1
b. 3
c. 3

Moroni 4
a. 3
b. 3

Moroni 5
a. 2
b. 2

Moroni 6
a. 2–3
b. 4
c. 5–6
d. 7
e. 9

Moroni 7
a. 3

b. 9
c. 10–11
d. 12
e. 13
f. 15–17
g. 17
h. 30
i. 31
j. 41
k. 45–47
l. 48

Moroni 8
a. Doctrine and
Covenants 29:47
b. Doctrine and
Covenants 65:25–
27
c. 24
d. 25
e. 25
f. 25
g. 26
h. 26
i. 27

Moroni 9
a. 3–5
b. 6, 25
c. 9
d. 19
e. 19
f. 21
g. 23
h. 25

Moroni 10
a. 1
b. 3–4
c. 5
d. 9–16
e. 17–18
f. 20–21
g. 22
h. 32–33
i. 34